LIFE IS A JOURNEY EMBRACE IT

DR RAJAN DESHPANDE

AF518718

BlueRose ONE.com
Stories Matter
NewDelhi • London

BLUEROSE PUBLISHERS
India | U.K.

Copyright © Dr. Rajan Deshpande 2025

All rights reserved by author. No part of this publication may be reproduced, stored in a retrieval system or transmitted in any form or by any means, electronic, mechanical, photocopying, recording or otherwise, without the prior permission of the author. Although every precaution has been taken to verify the accuracy of the information contained herein, the publisher assumes no responsibility for any errors or omissions. No liability is assumed for damages that may result from the use of information contained within.

BlueRose Publishers takes no responsibility for any damages, losses, or liabilities, that may arise from the use or misuse of the information, products, or services provided in this publication.

BlueRose ONE.com
Stories Matter
NewDelhi • London

For permissions requests or inquiries regarding this publication, please contact:

BLUEROSE PUBLISHERS
www.BlueRoseONE.com
info@bluerosepublishers.com
+91 8882 898 898
+4407342408967

ISBN: 978-93-7310-223-8

Cover design: Yash Singhal
Typesetting: Namrata Saini

First Edition: October 2025

This book is dedicated to my beloved

daughter Rasika, and daughter in law, Dr Pallavi,

the two shining stars in my life
who bring joy, love,

and happiness to my world.

डॉ. बी. एन. गंगाधर
अध्यक्ष
Dr. B. N. Gangadhar
Chairman

सत्यमेव जयते

आज़ादी का अमृत महोत्सव

राष्ट्रीय आयुर्विज्ञान आयोग
स्वास्थ्य एवं परिवार कल्याण मंत्रालय
भारत सरकार
National Medical Commission
Ministry of Health & Family Welfare
Government of India

FOREWORD

Life is a journey. We must live it; live it fully with life! All doctors may give more years to our life but people like Dr. Deshpande, the author of this book can give more life to those years. In this journey of our life, we often focus on the destination; a college, a job, a family, a house, etc. Do we energetically and happily lead the life in this journey? The book gives answers to this question. The author illustrates several situations in our life that can enliven us. The three chapters are on what do we learn in this journey, the God and personal experiences of the author in his medical practice.

Several examples and anecdotes are poignant and well animated. The message not only reaches our brains but also our hearts. An example how one should be a controlled person, be a 'Sthitapragna' focusing on your action, the Lord said in Bhagavad Geeta. The Ugandan experience exemplifies this.

Significance of parents' roles in bringing up the children is illustrated by two examples. One being positive, the other one being an oversight. Every parent has to be with the children as they are growing up and in their journey as well. As parents we can buffer their efforts, buttress their ascent. Let them feel good that they succeeded. Let us also appreciate roles others play in the upbringing of our children, a teacher perhaps. Small deeds produce profound effects. It just needs a right advice for doing a small but good deed. A warm hug gives a feeling of good (perhaps by releasing those feel-good hormones).

The unconditional faith children harbor is touching to note. The kid asks the cardiac surgeon to wish the God in her heart in the surgery. What an emotional situation? God is in us. Can we ensure we do his role of safeguarding dharma and keep the society harmonious?

Dr. Deshpande narrates the experience of setting up clinical practice, the travails of bringing this to excellence. His own journey as a medical practitioner, deservedly recognised for several awards, could be example to many. Several simple gestures of the dos and don'ts may not have figured in text books. Books mainly teach those that have been proven in evidence generating research. The experience has not been seen as a strong enough evidence.

Readers would benefit from this book not just as a refreshing read but as a resource of 'healthy' values that each of us including doctors will gain from adopting those in us.

Date : 07th July, 2025

Place : New Delhi

(DR. B.N.GANGADHAR) MD Dsc
Chairman, National Medical Commission,
Professor Emeritus Integrative Medicine
Former Senior Professor(Psychiatry) and Director(Retd.)
National Institute of Mental Health and Neuro Sciences (NIMHANS)
Bengaluru, Karnataka, India

Pocket-14, Sector-8, Phase-I, Dwarka, New Delhi-110077
Tele: 011-25367039, Website: www.nmc.org.in, Email: chairmanps@nmc.org.in

From The Author's Desk

Life is a journey of discovery, a jewel to be cherished and garment to be worn: Shiny Iris

Life is a journey! It is never a smooth sailing in anyone's life. It is always on a roller coaster. All individual encounter ups and downs in life. It is up to a person to encounter the difficult period and manage to take the journey forward. The downs in life are common and it is the art of bouncing back which is important. One needs to get elated when you are on an upbeat mood. With achievements one feels proud of life. However, this should not go to the head of anyone. The life is uncertain and unpredictable. What is in store for the future cannot be predicted by anyone. Hence, it is of paramount importance to be level-headed and, take their achievements, rewards and, awards in the right spirit. These should never change an attitude of a person.

Similarly, one may come across various downs in life and at times it takes longer time to come out of it. Such type of drawbacks in life hits a person badly and may slow down the growth in the path of journey. There are bad memories, instances and incidences which make a person not only sad but even depressed. These thoughts of bad memories are like a log. Majority of us carry these forwards in life on our shoulders or on the back. That makes the journey tough going because of the heavy load which we carry. These certainly slows down the speed further and it is ideal that this heavy stuff of the past should be left then and their only and move on in the journey with newer thinking, newer enthusiasm, and higher spirit. During the journey of life every moment teaches us something new. Learning is an art, go on enriching yourself with the experiences while you tread the right path.

Life's journey can be comparable to a train journey. Once we embark upon the train of life, the last stop is a place from where we leave this world. Like in the train, at every stop we get a new passenger, who may sit along with us, and you may find them amazing or interesting and few others may be distressing. You may like some or dislike others, but you should get going without your choice. Similarly in our life we can come across people who guide, assist, and help us and make us happy and teach us how to make others happy. On the other side there are many who criticise, talk ill, and put you down. Be smart enough and avoid such acquisition coolly.

That is the beauty of life, and we should enjoy the ride every moment. Life is short and it takes time to make good friends than creating enemies and feel sad and distressed. One, needs to learn to see best in everyone. Remember there is no one who permanently travels with us, except the close family members that too few for a little longer time. Even parents step out at some point of time. It is strange to find people who enjoy troubling others.

Life is short and we never have too much time for gladdening the hearts of those who are travelling the dark journey with us. Oh, be swift to love, make haste to be kind: ***Henri Frederic Amiel***

Our journey is filled with joy, sorrow, dreams and goodbyes. We truly do not know which station we ourselves going to disembark. So, one should live happily, learn to love and forgive before we step out, we need to leave beautiful memories for those who continue their journey. One should thank God for allowing us to board the train of life for the incredible journey.

We need to get adjusted well and understand others and never try to find fault with others that makes the life more beautiful. Life is an enjoyable affair, and no one should shed tears. But try to wipe the tears, who are at times in helpless and hopeless condition.

This is yet another book on "Life series." Many chapters have been picked up from my personal, family, or professional experience. In my seven decades of personal life and five decades of professional life, I have learnt many good things and newer experiences which I have depicted in this book. There are few other chapters which I have picked up from discussions with others and so also after reading or listening to others.

I do not claim to own them as my own. They have excellent messages for life and hence they are incorporated into this book which may make a slight difference in the life of readers. Good thoughts should spread to many and should help them to improve their own lives to make the journey of life a better one.

I would like to express my sincere gratitude to my dear friend, Dr Dilip Malhotra, for his time and effort in proofreading this book. His positive feedback and insightful suggestions were instrumental in making this book more reader friendly.

I have no words to express my gratitude to Shri Padmashri Dr B N Gangadhar for his excellent and wonderful foreword. His words have added immense value to my work and have enriched it.

Life is a journey, and every chapter covered should be interesting. It is a journey that we must learn to savour, cherish, and treasure.

Joy is found not in finishing an activity but doing it.

- Greg Anderson

Life is a journey that has lot of different paths. But any path one chooses, use it as destiny. Friends, Focus on the journey not the destination.

I am the master of my fate, and I am the captain of my boat. While ups and downs are a part of everyone's journey, how you face it makes you the person or artiste you are: Jubin Nautiyal

Contents

CHAPTER I

LOTS TO LEARN FROM LIFE

Uneducated Father's Highly Educated Children

MATRU DEVO BHAVA

Rampur was a taluka place; a well irrigated place and the main economy was from agriculture. There were many farm owners with large agricultural lands. The town had school, college, and taluka Panchayat, tehsildar office. It was not a flourishing town but a sleepy one.

Shambhu Gouda was a progressive farmer and inherited agricultural land and continued to cultivate crops as his ancestors were doing. He never stepped into any school and thus was an uneducated one. Whether his parents had not sent him to school, or he had no interest in it was not known. Though dark-skinned, he had a good personality. A six-footer with a well-built body and imposing moustache made him a young, handsome man. His only grouse was that he did not have formal education. However, he had profound common sense and wisdom to forge ahead in the life. He decided to marry an educated lady as his dream was to educate his children well.

Thus, Triveni, a schoolteacher, came into his life. She agreed to marry him as he was handsome and had big agricultural lands to support his income. In the present-day circumstances, girls want an educated boy but in arranged marriages parents look beyond the job and prefer a boy with sound financial background. Triveni agreed as parents convinced her about the boy, but she herself liked the smart young well-built man.

Triveni's influence transformed Shambhu Gouda's life.

She revolutionised traditional farming with modern techniques. She, along with Shambhu, went to District headquarters discussed with agricultural and horticultural experts and sought their help. Several types of modern equipment were introduced. Drip irrigation and bore well made a lot of difference to the yield. The land was converted to horticulture including fruit-bearing trees.

Shambu was really a blessed one by bringing an educated girl into the family. In the meantime, they were blessed with a baby girl. The happiness of the couple soared high, and they named her 'Asha' as she was the hope for the family. As she was growing, the couple planned for the second baby in the hope of getting a male child. They were not lucky, and the second baby girl was named Neeta.

With Triveni's care and proper upbringing, both girls were doing well in school.

It was their dream to see Asha as an IAS officer.

In the meantime, Shambhu wanted to go for the third child to have a male child to inherit his huge property. Triveni summarily rejected it and said a flat

"NO." She said what would happen if we got another girl. She would be an unwanted child. I am not for it. Forget it said Triveni. After all, she was an educated wife. He had to snub his dream as he knew that he would not win an argument with her.

They continued their focus on both two brilliant girls.

Triveni herself taught them science and maths. They passed their SSLC with flying colours, and Asha stood first in the state.

Both decided to send them to the best of the college in the District Headquarters. They arranged a PG (paying guest) in a family known to them.

Parents had planted their desire to see Asha as an IAS officer. It was deeply rooted in her, too, and she also started dreaming about it. However, she preferred to finish engineering first and simultaneously started preparing in that direction. After completing engineering, she went to Delhi to get training. She could crack the UPSC exams to get high rank and, fortunately, got the Karnataka cadre. It was an immense joy for the family, and they were on "cloud 9."

The second girl was also equally brilliant, and parents had not put their thoughts for her for her future. She was independent, and she too was ambitious person even though she was fun-loving and happy go lucky.

She had made up her mind to be a police officer. She was pretty impressed by the lady Superintendent of Police who had come as the chief guest for the annual gathering. The dress or uniform she wore and her stance and the way she walked and her jeep and assistants around her made an impact on her mind. She took her autograph and had a photograph with her. She followed her dream and cleared IPS to serve in the police department. She, too, was fortunately, posted to Karnataka cadre.

Triveni and Shambhu Gouda reached the pinnacle of happiness.

By this time, Triveni was the principal of the school. As everything was going smoothly, there came an unexpected turning point in their life.

Both Shambhu Gouda and Triveni were in a fix. All decisions were usually made jointly, and with mutual understanding. This was a crucial one. Unexpectedly Triveni was pregnant. She was ashamed of herself, and it was not the time to have a child when her own daughters were of marriageable age.

Lot of discussion went for a couple of days without any conclusion.

Shambhu felt it was God's gift. He appealed to her, telling her it is certainly a gift of God and killing our own child is sin. When you said no to my request. when we were young, I conceded to your request. But now, I know it is not the age but let us not abort. His eyes could tell that he was begging for it. Finally, they agreed to go ahead of it. They had to face humiliation in the society. On top of it, her own officer children, both Asha & Neeta, had no words to tell dad, but said to mom that she could have aborted. Triveni felt shy and said that "your dad said that it is God's gift."

She delivered a baby boy, and this brought an end to their period of humiliation.

Both Asha & Neeta were happy to see their little brother.

The third child was different as he received more love affection and was a pampered child. Both parents who were busy with their vocations. Triveni was the principal, and Shambu was a social activist. Their attention to their son Vivek was limited. Vivek was too good in sports. His favourite sports were kabaddi, kho-kho, and basketball. Apart from that he was a great debater with lot of common sense and general knowledge. However, his interest in academics was taking a back seat.

He was not properly guided, and, as a result, he was not at all doing well. Teachers brought it to the notice of Principal Triveni. They also said he was in bad company and that it would be good to put Vivek in a sports school. If he continues here, he will become a spoiled brat.

Triveni was shocked and discussed with her daughter Asha.

Asha could understand the problem and immediately shifted him to a good residential school where she was working. Asha never missed going to see him during the weekends. She also brought him to her quarters and counselled him every day. Age difference between two was so much that she was like his mother and used to put her hands around his shoulder and give him tips.

She told him nicely and emphasized that unless you establish your identity in society, no one will bother about you. Parents' grace will be there for only sometime. You should not be known as son of so and so. Instead, people should identify your parents as your father or mother. Be on your own. She used to tell him that it would be difficult for him to survive in the present world unless he was educated.

Study well with full attention without any diversions. She further said, "Continue with sports and debates in which you are good, but not at the cost of studies."

These were the pearls of wisdom.

These had profound impact on Vivek, and he changed his lifestyle and started focusing on studies.

He was not keen to do IAS, IPS, or anything like engineering or medicine. His interest was to have a factory and opted for a diploma in engineering, which he completed successfully.

He started a factory in his own town and established himself well, as he was a smart young man like his dad and was also hard working. He made big strides and made his products saleable, and thus, he was an entrepreneur of repute.

Vivek received lots of help and assistance from his classmate Dilip, who was a PA to the local MLA, Mr Kumar. During his leisure, he used to meet his friend Dilip. Eventually he used to meet the MLA Kumar also. He was the one who had inaugurated his start up factory. MLA was a young man who liked Vivek and asked him for his help during elections. He moved with him the length and breadth of the constituency. Vivek, a good orator right from his school days, impressed the audience. Kumar won the election with a huge margin. In the meantime, Vivek came across many party leaders. He was liked for his pleasing manners and industrious nature. He was a grass root worker for the party. He was not only successful in his industry but also had a big name in society.

The next elections were slated in another four months. There were many preliminary meetings, and Vivek was a part of it.

It so happened that as MLA Kumar was heading for a party meeting, he met with a bad accident. Unfortunately, despite the doctors' best efforts, he did not survive. It was a great shock to his PA, Dilip, and Vivek. It took a long time to come out of it.

When the next choice for the party post was discussed, Vivek's name came to the forefront. As party leaders were well acquainted with him and knew his potential and capabilities. As he knew everyone in the constituency, it was easy for him to get elected.

A vagabond boy who was poor in his studies could become a leader. He knew it was because of his sister Asha. He held her in high esteem and respected her a lot. When the election results were announced, he went straight to her, hugged her, and touched her feet.

Fortune laughed at the third child of Triveni & Shambhu

All three children were well settled by grace of God, Uneducated Shambhu Gowda's dream came into reality. Triveni played a significant role in it.

Asha was posted as a District Collector, and Neeta as Superintendent of Police.

Neeta always felt proud of Asha as a senior officer in the district.

As the days passed, Neeta was promoted as DIG and posted to Bengaluru and similarly Asha took the charge as the horticultural Secretary, in the Government.

When the General elections were held, and popular MLA Vivek won easily, and he was fortunate to be the minister for Industries.

It was a strange coincidence that Asha, the principal secretary to Industries, was working under her brother Vivek.

Whenever she had to meet him in the chamber, she used to send a chit with her name.

Vivek was a modest person with all humility used to go to the door and welcome her. He never sat on his chair and preferred to sit along with her to discuss to work out plans.

He never forgot to offer coffee and went up to the door to open himself.

Once he was invited for an inauguration of an industry. Neeta oversaw the bandobast. As the minister entered, she saluted him. It was embarrassing for him, but he saluted in return and with folded hands bowed down and said namaste and patted her on the back, keeping up the protocols at the same time expressed his humility.

During festivals, all the family used to meet. Even though Triveni and Shambhu Gowda were old they preferred to stay in their own home. That was a great get-together of successful children in life and dreamer parents.

Parents should have dreams for their children and make all efforts to tread the path to reach that goal.

A mother always plays a pivotal role in a family, and a good mother with a clear vision, like Triveni, can make all the difference.

Here, it correctly implies as "Matru Devo Bhava" meaning the mother is equal to God. It is said that God could not be everywhere and so He created mothers. What an apt statement.

Shambhu was also visionary and a dreamer. Had he married a village girl, what would have happened, God only knows.!! He decided to marry an educated lady, which had influence in his life.

Visionary parents with obedient, hardworking, principled children with a distinct goal will make life better and meaningful.

LIVE WITH HOPE, FOLLOW YOUR DREAM WITH PASSION,

NOTHING STOPS YOU FROM BECOMING SUCESSFUL.

LIFE IS A CHALLENGE FACE IT WITH DETERMINATION.

Sacrifice

Life is a song, sing it. Life is a game play it.
Life is a challenge, meet it. Life is a dream realize it.
Life is a sacrifice offer it. Life is love enjoy it

Sai Baba

In life, we come across true stories or happenings wherein sacrifices of a person galore. Similarly, gratitude and happiness in helping others is also equally seen in many instances. However, presently, these values have been eroded sufficiently in every human life, and everything gets concentrated and revolves around themselves. They do not see beyond self. If anything must happen then it should be of some personal benefit otherwise that work will never happen. Thus, unfortunately we do see children abandoning their own parents who have toiled hard to bring them up. They coolly say that they have done their job, which they are supposed to do and nothing beyond. These are truly ungrateful people.

However, there are instances of families following the traditional values. This is a story of such a couple. It is not a story of a particular family and if it coincides with someone it could be just a coincidence and without prejudice to anyone, the story is depicted.

Raghunandan was a company secretary and was a powerful person in the management of a big industry. His wife Madhu was post graduate in social science and preferred not to work but instead started the social cause. Both were happily married. Yes, truly, and not like the one wherein somebody introduces a couple as "They are happily married" or "Made for each other"

In fact, many a time, they are not happy in their post marriage days, nor they are made for each other. On the contrary they never get along well in their home with each other's idiosyncrasies. However, Madhu and Raghunandan had ultimate happiness and perfect understanding and mutual respect. The only thing that was bothering them that they had no issues. There was no place where they had not been. They visited all the temples, Gurudwaras and even mosques as they were truly secular. They had not left any babas, spiritual gurus or religious heads. Both being educated they knocked the doors of leading doctors too. That is how Gods, Goddesses photos found a place in their drawing room. Both husband and wife never went out of their house without bowing their heads and praying to God for their blessings. The frames were cleaned properly, dusted and Kumkum was placed on forehead of all the Gods every day.

These massive prayers and medication from doctors and blessings of Gurus worked and Madhu got pregnant. They had a baby boy who was healthy and looking pretty. They left no stone unturned to take care of his health and upbringing. The house was full of toys and as the boy grew up and all that he demanded was immediately brought in. He was not only loved but also pampered. The boy grew up to be a handsome man and had a fair complexion which he got from his mother and particularly good at everything which he got from the father's side.

As the only son they named him Jestavardhana. As the days passed, he went to a well-known school in the city. Parents were busy making strides in their own business and social field. Raghunandan was then the vice president of the company and had absolutely no time for anything. He had to attend meeting after meetings and often travelled abroad for company's work. He had no time to see what is going on in the house. His personal attention for his lovely son also lessened. Similarly, his wife Madhu who was into social service became the president of a couple of organisations in the city. Being a good organiser and an orator, she also got several posts at the State level. She too was leaving the house early and coming late or going to State headquarter leaving the house to her assistant. The photos of Gods and Goddesses and flower decorated frames had all vanished. There was pile of dust on those photographs and nobody had time to clean it or worship as their only wish of getting the son was fulfilled.

Whenever Jestavardhana stood first in the class and came home running to share this great news with his parents in anticipation of a hug from dad and a kiss from mom was shattered when nothing of that kind happened. Both were well dressed, dad in a 3-piece suit and mom in a costly silk saree with jewellery and makeup they were about to leave for the function and their hug, or a kiss would have spoiled their attire. The boy who came jumping with a great joy being 1st in the class was told by his dad, 'well done I too used to be 1st and keep it up. Mother just patted and they went off. Jestavardhana felt bad and was sad. The young man's big dream of love of parents was shattered by the shabby way his parents treated him.

As the parents were not there most of the time and food was prepared by the housemaids and most of his time went into talking to maids than parents. He was grown into "Ayaa /maid culture" and picked up her language and sometimes abuses. He was addicted to mobile and TV and naturally his concentration on studies came down. Unfortunately, this was never noticed by parents during their busy schedule. As a result of all this, Jestavardhana the topper of the class slipped down drastically and his classmate, his teacher's son got his place. Despite that parents' eyes never opened as they were in their own eutopia. However, his teacher who had seen the brilliant and smart child going down in his rankings and studies felt for him. His son and Jestavardhana were close friends. They both shared their feelings. The teacher understood the reason for his downfall. Finally, the kind-hearted teacher felt that this brilliant child will go astray if not picked up at this stage. He took the courage and went to Jestavardhana's parents. In his humble way, he told the father "Sir, your son is a brilliant student and for some reason he is not performing well. My son, Raman is his classmate and a friend. I tutor my son at home and if you permit, I can also tutor your son along with him. He further added that he does not expect any monetary considerations for this. I will love teaching him. Teacher was intelligent that rich parents may think him otherwise and made it clear that it will be for free and left no ambiguity. This came as a bolt from the blue to both Raghunandan and Madhu. They had no other option and readily agreed to this offer.

This is exactly what happens many times in this new age parenting while they go up the ladder in their own professions and vocation. Their attention to their children is not same as it used to be earlier. They are extremely happy in their own fields with laurels bestowed upon them for their achievements. If the child fails to perform, they do not mind giving huge donations to send their wards to medical, engineering or any college for that matter. The sacred thread of love, affection, affinity with parents is thus separated or cut easily. Thus, in turn, children will not have any respect for their parents. Then, parents have no right to demand respect. The generation gap widens deeply. Jestavardhana started his tuitions at his teacher's house. Teacher was humble; he had a small house with a bedroom, kitchen and drawing room. He had a second-hand scooter. He enjoyed teaching. He taught his son and Jestavardhana with same affinity. His wife was giving them milk with bournvita as a regular feature. Both Jesta and Raman were studying together. Teacher had taken Jesta as his foster son. Many a time, he also used to have dinner at teacher's house, whenever his parents were out of station. The intimacy with his teacher and his wife Rukmini grew as the days passed on.

Jesta wanted to be a CA (chartered accountant), whereas Raman, the teacher's son wanted to pursue his studies in music. He was good in music, had a particularly good voice and was going for sitar and tabla classes too. He got many prizes in school competition and at the State level competition. His parents were so considerate that they never forced him to be a doctor, lawyer, or an engineer. They allowed him to pursue his passion. Likewise, Jesta continued his studies towards his aim of becoming a CA. As the teacher predicted, he did very well and passed CA exam in his first attempt which is not so easy. Likewise, he started his practice and settled down well.

Raman started as music teacher in the college and started his own classes in music. As he was an excellent vocalist, he was invited to many functions, his popularity increased day by day and he also performed at some of the crucial functions wherein Chief Minister and Governor were present. He was the most sought-after vocalist and sitarist. He was also sent abroad for concerts and wherein he won the hearts of the public. Thus, in a brief time he was a very well-known musician not only at the State but also at the National level. As a CA, Jesta was doing very well and was attached to many of the corporates and professionally very well known. Once Raman settled down well, he never forgot to take Jesta, his good friend to special concerts and take his feedback too.

Jesta had suffered with jaundice whilst in the college. He was hospitalised for many days. He was quite serious. His parents, especially the mother, made it a point to see him regularly and attend to him. However, his teacher and his wife were sleeping with him in the night and were available 24X7 at his service and so was his dear friend Raman. He came out of the death bed and recovered well. He was given advice regarding his diet, dos and don'ts and strictly warned not to touch alcohol. By God's grace he recovered fully well.

Both friends were doing well in their own professions and vocations. After couple of years, Jestavardhana's health started deteriorating and the specialist doctors who examined him suggested that his liver was not functioning well and so he may require a liver transplant if he must survive. It was a rude shock for the whole family. He was born after many prayers and after perambulations to many temples and reaching out to gurus and expert doctors. The impact was very bad on the teacher who was a foster father and loved him very much. Doctors said it would be nice if a relative can donate the liver. It may not be the full liver but part of liver to be transplanted as the liver grows on its own from the donor. Both parents started worrying about it. Though he was their own son they were selfish and not ready to part away with their liver. After series of discussion amongst themselves they request Doctors to get donor liver. Doctor explained to them that it is not easy for a cadaver liver transplant because chances of rejections are high. It would be preferable if somebody is ready to have organ donation soon after death and there may be long waiting period. Parents were reluctant and said they did not mind waiting. In the meantime, his friend Raman came forward to donate his liver to his good friend. He had got all the preliminary investigations done without Jesta's knowledge and he was found to be a perfect match for the donation. When this came to Jesta's knowledge, he flatly refused. "I do not want you to compromise with your life. I prefer dying rather than getting your liver as I want you to lead normal complete life". Raman was frustrated; there was a great silence in both the families. Everybody particularly in the Teacher's family were in tears with dark clouds swirling around them. How long would he live if a donor was not found, was on everybody's minds. In the meantime, Raman had talked to the doctor and was ready to offer his liver anytime. Doctors too counselled Jestavardhana to accept his liver but he was adamant.

In the meantime, Raman got an offer to give a performance at Ravindra Kalakshetra, Bangalore for an important State level function where the Chief Minister was the Chief Guest. There were many stalwarts, Union minister, bureaucrats, top judiciary people, and celebrities were to be present. Raman was in two minds and when he shared this with his friend, Jesta asked him to go ahead as it was a wonderful opportunity. I would not die before you come, he said. Go and perform well and come back. Jesta's words "Do well, impress well" were ringing in his ears. His performance was superb and enthralling. Chief Minister did enquire whether, he had received any Rajyotsava Award any time and then suggested Kannada Cultural Minister to propose his name. Raman was elated and started his return journey in the car provided by the Government. Everyone in family including Jesta witnessed live performance on television. They too were super exited; they were waiting to receive him after bringing laurels. Raman was returning to his native land. His speeding car was in collision with a truck. The driver and the passenger sitting in the front died on the spot and Raman sustained multiple injuries including head injury. He was immediately shifted to the Government Hospital and then to the medical college. This was truly a tragic accident. In the medical college the expert doctors after thorough examination declared him brain dead. By that time all the family members were in medical hospital. Everyone was shattered and unconsolable. The news reached the doctor who was treating Jestavardhana. He knew that he was fit to give his liver when he was alive and then felt this is the right opportunity for a friend who is brain dead to donate his liver to his ailing friend and make his life comfortable. By doing this, his friend's liver will be in his body and thus his parents, teacher and wife will be happy. Finally, after counselling the parents, they happily agreed for donation of liver from brain dead Raman. Thus, all arrangements were made for the transplantation. On one side there was mourning and on the other side a sort of satisfaction that Raman will live on in the body of his friend Jesta.

Jestavardhana, a smart young man was all set to get operated and there was a duty doctor who felt pity on him and took lot of personal care and counselled him after surgery and said that he can lead a normal life. She also gave example of many such patients who were doing well. If there is any iota of doubt about rejection of the liver, she made it clear, your friend Raman had done all the test possible, and he was a perfect match, but you rejected it when he was alive. You are lucky to get the same person's liver and that too from a friend whose all parameters matched perfectly. You will lead a normal life. Do not worry. Further, she said, think positive in life. The depressed Jesta brightened up with hope and was all set to undergo operation with confidence. Post operative, the same duty doctor by name Dr. Deepa took care of him as she was posted in the ICU and her advice gave him a lot of confidence. He recovered fast without any complications. Dr. Deepa was deeply impressed by his personality and his talks. She started liking him but had no courage to tell him, as he was still recovering. Jestavardhana was discharged and he thanked every staff in the hospital while he held the hands of Dr. Deepa and thanked her for being with him to give courage and confidence. She said that he was fit to go home, and to follow the medical instructions. She knew that she loved him and as they were parting, she said they would meet sometime to which he nodded. Later, after his recovery they managed to meet in a place, and she confided in him and told him that she is in love with him. Though he liked her, knowingly well his position he was not keen to go ahead with it. He just said that he needed some time to think, and then onwards this thought started brooding in his mind. On one hand he was passionate about her love and probably she was the perfect match, but on the other hand he was hesitant because he was not certain about the days ahead of him after the liver transplant despite every body's assurance that he will lead a normal full life.

Dr. Deepa was none other than the daughter of the surgeon who did the liver transplant, but her love story was not known to him. One day she decided to talk it over and found a suitable time when her father was free. She said that she would like to marry Jesta, as she was in love with him. Father was shocked and said "what are you talking about" you know the uncertainty of liver transplant. How can I allow you to marry him. I know all the consequences myself and cannot get my daughter to marry him. Deepa was upset, looked in his eye and said, "Have you not told him that he can lead normal and full life and so also I gave him the same moral courage." Do you think you have given him false notation? If you think complications are bound to be there, then you have lied to him." Her father said what I told is truth, but it may not happen all the time. The girl was bold enough to ask her dad to presume she had a liver transplant, and he had offered his hand to me what you would have done? There was a big silence and father cooled down but asked to her to rethink and went off. There was no question of rethinking in her mind as she was very firm. On the other side Jestavardhana was not very comfortable marrying a doctor that too a liver transplant surgeon's daughter who otherwise would get a good healthy person as her husband instead of him.

Despite Dr. Deepa persuading him and convincing him about her love and desire to marry him, he was not budging. Deepa's father, who was initially reluctant, subsequently agreed and went to Jestavardhana, put his hand over his shoulder, and said that he needed a big favour from him. Then he said that his daughter Deepa loves him so much that she had broken her engagement with a cardiac surgeon for getting married to you. I will be too happy to have you as my son in law. Kindly accept it, it will be blessing on my child. Finally, Jesta agreed as he could not say no to surgeon who has given life and the lady who gave all her love.

The wedding was done in simple manner with small group of relatives, but a grand reception was arranged where many well-known personalities were in attendance. It was surprising to note that many noted musicians of the country were there to greet the couple. They all could see musical gentlemen Raman in Jestavardhana. There was a long queue where in people lined up to greet the couple. Jesta got down from the stage, went to the audience where the Teacher and his wife Rukmini were seated. He bowed down, touched their feet took their blessings and escorted them back to stage. The entire crowd greeted the newlyweds and congratulated the Teacher couple. Jestavardhana's real parents, Raghunandan and his wife Madhu were side lined and did not receive any importance while the teacher and his wife were on the spotlight.

Raghunandan and his wife who were busy with their own lives realised their mistake but were happy that their son came out good against all odds with the teacher's blessing and help.

Such things happen in many families where children are deprived of parent's attention and go astray. They may not study, become a vagabond or turn into anti-social elements. They are not only lost to parents but also to society. However, in Jesta's life things were different as his teacher stood like a rock and moulded his personality and make him a fine human being. Friendship of Raman and Jesta is a role model. It is not the money that plays a key role but the warmth, love, affection, and empathy that makes a significant difference in the life of anyone and so was so in the life of Jestavardhana.

Organ donation is the best donation in life. One may donate millions of rupees for any cause, but it cannot be compared with any organ donation. Likewise, Jesta's life was full of eternal love and affection from a person who was not related to him.

This was a story of profound sacrifices by the teacher's family and that of his friend Raman. Similarly, the doctor's deep love and her father, despite being fully aware of the difficulties of the transplants consented to his daughter's marriage. This act speaks volumes of true love and sacrifice.

A family which has a peace of mind, love in the heart and warmth in the hands and who share the happiness and manage the ups and downs at every moment in a right spirit to sail the lifeboat smoothly crossing all the odds and reaching the shore will certainly make a perfect family.

A family who lives together

Eats together.

Prays together and

Understands each other.

is a blessed family which enjoys long time togetherness, contentment, and happiness.

A MAN WHO WAS COMPLETELY INNOCENT, OFFERED HIMSELF AS A SACRIFICE FOR GOOD OF OTHERS INCLUDING HIS ENEMIES AND BECAME THE RANSOM OF THE WORLD. IT WAS A PERFECT ACT

Mahatma Gandhi

It Is Not the Complexion but The Spirit Within That Makes a Difference

Life is all the colours!

Those who have darkness in mind turn their bodies in darkness as well.

Life is colourful: be like a rainbow, use every colour: Do not get stuck with one colour, be colourful!!

Kaveri was the only daughter of Manjunath Swami and Parimala. Manjunath Swami popularly known as Manju was a leading businessman in the town. He was highly respected in the community because of his goodness and lot of philanthropy which he was doing. His wife Parimala who was popularly addressed as Pari was a beautiful lady. However, Manjunath swamy was pitch dark in colour but well-built and smart to look at and his behaviour and attitudes were excellent. Except for his dark colour he was perfect. Their togetherness was so good that they hardly fought for any reason.

Pari was pregnant and the couple took temple run asking every God to give a beautiful child with mother's colour. Both wanted a baby girl, and they were blessed with one. The baby was very fair and looking probably better than her mom. It was a happy family and enjoyed their time together.

Later the couple decided to have a second baby. This time their wish was to have a son. Like the last time they visited many temples. They never asked about the colour like they did the last time.

The baby was born. God had not granted their wish. It was a baby girl again, but she had a pitch-dark complexion. Parents were utterly disappointed and worried. Both started discussing about what they felt. They had no issues with having another girl but were not happy with the dark complexion.

It was inevitable and they went on nurturing the child. However, the pet remained the first one.

The first baby was named as Spoorti and second one Keerti.

Both the kids started growing together and later started going to school.

Even Spoorti was hesitant to accompany her younger sister as she was dark. In the house Keerti did hear talking about her colour. Mother used to take the first girl to parties leaving the second girl at home.

This worked on the small little girl, and she was feeling bad. On one side mother was showing the same love and affection what she showed to Spoorti. On the other hand, Spoorti always tried to avoid her, just because she was dark. Keerti was always tearful because of this. The poor girl could not express it to anyone.

Even in school, other kids used to tease them as "Gora and Kala" meaning 'fair and dark'.

With these comments, Keerti used to be aloof and hardly had few friends.

The dark colour was working on her mind. She always felt that she was an unwanted child. She was going into depression. Whom to tell? Who will understand her feelings?

The first one Spoorti was a favourite of teachers too because of her pretty looks.

The language teacher Mr Surendranath was observing this keenly. Keerti really had good looks and physic. Except for her colour she was excellent. Surendranath took pity on her and started talking to her and understanding her and her worries. He won her confidence. He knew the family well, but he knew that talking to parents would not help. Fortunately, his daughter was Keerit's classmate.

Once he called Keerti to his house after taking permission of her parents.

He put his hand over her shoulder and said, "I am like your father". I find you alone, not mixing up and not interacting with others. What is the reason? Initially she said everything was OK. That is my nature she said.

As a counsellor he straight away asked her whether her colour was bothering her? She looked down and kept quiet. Later, she started crying loudly. The teacher has spotted the right reason for her withdrawal.

Then he promised that that he would help her and see that a smart girl like her can do anything in life. "You have all the qualities to fly high in the sky."

Colour is not the one that will take you high. It is your talent and positive spirit that makes the difference. I shall see that all students will flock around you. This is my promise to you said Surendranath, the teacher. This was a ray of hope for Keerti. Her eyes brightened and smile appeared on her face which had disappeared for a long time.

Teacher Surendranath took personal interest and started training her for debate and elocution competitions. Being a bright girl, she picked it up. The "I can do Spirit " instilled by her teacher did work in a positive way.

She started involving herself in the competition. With teacher's training she performed extremely well. She started getting prizes in school. Other teachers picked her up for inter school competition where again she got prizes. She then became the favourite of schoolteachers. She represented the school at District level and got medals. She represented her school at state level competition and won the trophy.

By this time, she was the most sought-after student at the school. Even principal appreciated her in open assembly and gatherings. Her photographs and write- ups appeared in the daily magazine.

Even the attitude of parents changed, and they could understand where they failed.

They only concentrated on her colour and not merit. Such a brilliant student was discarded as useless. She was the most liked student at the school.

Spoorti who was hesitant to walk along with her because of her colour started saying that she is her younger sister which most of the students were not aware of.

This was one side of personality. The other side was her passion for sports. Looking at her good physic, Surendranath (the teacher) had introduced her to the PE teacher. She took a lot of interest in two sports, cricket and football.

She was exceptionally good in both. Looking at her performance she was specially trained in both these sports.

She was an all-rounder in Cricket. She represented in under-17 cricket at State level. She was too good in it reached dizzy heights. She was the heart throb, and she later represented at the national level in cricket. She was by that time a celebrity.

Spoorti was also good in her studies and opted to be a chartered accountant. She completed with flying colours.

Manjunath Swami and Parimala arranged her wedding in a big way.

It was surprising that most of the invitees greeted the beautiful Spoorti, but keen to meet Keerti, spend time with her and pictures taken with Keerti the celebrity.

Thus, the colour made no difference and at this hour a dark coloured girl was on the hot spot.

Both parents looking at her success and popularity felt ashamed of themselves as they had discarded her because of her colour. They never ever imagined that one day this dark coloured girl will bring laurels to the family.

As far as Keerti is concerned nothing went to her head she had all the respect for her parents and lots of love for her elder sister Spoorti and engaged in all the preparations of the wedding.

In the meantime, there came a proposal from a national cricketer who too had a big-name all-over India and at international level. She humbly put the proposal to her parents and got their approval. As her fiancé was there in the town, he too wanted to meet the parents.

Keerti took him to her parents and to her Godfather, her teacher Surendranath. They touched his feet and hugged him tight, and tears started flowing from both profusely.

Then she said to her fiancé that this Guru is responsible for what I am today. I cannot pay him back enough in this Janam.

During the wedding, along with parents, Surendranath was also standing throughout and greeting everyone.

It is apt and clear that skin colour is not at all important to achieve anything in life. In the journey of life, it is the duty of parents to equate all children on a same platform. Colour, qualifications, money, positions should not have any impact.

For parents, all children should be the same.

Some may be beautiful, and others may not be so or even ugly. Some will earn more and some less. Some will be achievers and some others ordinary.

But it should not bring disparity. The love and affection of parents is immeasurable, and it cannot be quantified.

Every child has equal right to receive their share of love and care in abundance from their parents.

God gives you precious stones. Making them shine is the responsibility of parents.

In an equivalent way it is the teacher who can have influence in the lives of children.

It is like what the language teacher Surendranath could find in a child and gave her right direction to go up the ladder of success.

Likewise, teachers should be looking beyond routine teaching and spot weaknesses and help the students to make a way to success. All children are like precious stones. It is up to the society, the teachers, and parents to make them shine.

Skin colour gives wrong message to onlookers. It does not show the true colour of an individual. External appearance is often deceptive. Inner potential is not evident to the naked eye. The potential in a human being has tremendous capacity to recharge and resound with ultimate success.

God gives the wisdom to parents to know what is right and wrong and the difference between the two.

Children should never feel that they are unwanted by their parents or even teachers. This mentality of parents works on the growing brain and is deeply rooted and will have long lasting impact. Parenteral responsibility is tremendous, and they should unearth the potential in their child. Emotional intelligence plays a vital role. Some children may be good in studies while others in arts, sports, extracurricular and cultural activities. These do not come under the preview of the syllabus. Parents should put a large canvas in front of children and allow them to shine in the field of their choice. They should never narrow down the choice to their liking. Marks may not be the only criteria to shine in this world, and it is a myth. Keep the options wide open and support and encourage children.

Many children who may be poor in studies have tremendous common sense and manage the life courageously. At no time colour of a person should come in the way of progress in life.

INNER POTENTIALS ARE NOT DEPICTED IN THE OUTSIDE COLOUR!

Distractions, Attractions, Drift Kids

You can't improve a wrong path by trying to walk better or faster or smarter. Get on a right path.

Henry Cloud

Ramanna was a small-time farmer, and his wife was Sitamma, a home maker. They had a small farm where Jawar was grown. It was good enough for both. They were fortunate to have a son. Their joy could not be measured and Ramanna popularly known in the village as Ramu went on hugging everyone he met and shared his joy.

Both Ramu and Sitamma had a dream to educate their son and make him an officer. As a farmer he always respected learned people who were officers.

Their son Ravi obtained his primary education in the village itself.

Teachers always complimented parents for having a brilliant kid. Ravi was sent to high school at the district headquarter where many students studied.

Fortunately, there was no need for a hostel as Ramu's younger brother was a clerk in Revenue Department. He had a daughter who was studying in the fourth grade. Even he had a dream to see Ravi as an officer. He wanted him to be an IAS or IPS officer.

As a brilliant student Ravi was doing very well and fully focussed on curricular activities. He had the goal to get good grades. He used to come straight home after the school hours.

He passed the SSLC exams with flying colours and secured state ranking too. He continued his further education in a reputed college. Being brilliant and focused he got the best rank in PUC 2nd year.

Now the time came for the decision making. His uncle wanted him to pursue his dream of IAS. His father being uneducated said " My son' I have no idea which course you need to choose. I can only say to get into a line where you can enjoy your profession. After a long thought and after discussing with his teachers and friends he decided to go for engineering. He never wanted to disappoint his uncle and said to him "Dear uncle, I shall have basic engineering degree first and later, attempt for IAS".

He got an admission in a well-known engineering college.

As the town was a little far away, he preferred to stay in the hostel which was attached to the college. Parents and his uncle were happy and thrilled.

Father Ramu very rarely visited the hostel, but Ravi used to come home during holidays.

He completed his classes and was to start final exams. Ravi used to take the blessings of his parents before writing exams by touching their feet. However, this time nothing of that kind happened. Ramu knew the dates of exams and wished him on phone assuming that his son must be busy in preparing for the examination.

The D Day of the results came. It was the shock of his lifetime for the poor farmer that his son Ravi had failed in the first year BE exam. How can this happen was, Ravi's dad's question. This was not anticipated by any stretch of his imagination.

He along with his brother went to his hostel room and met Ravi.

My dear son "what happened"? Anything wrong from our side? Were you not well? You should have asked us to come if you had problems."

So many questions to Ravi by his father who was sad. His uncle too enquired as to what went wrong.

Nothing came out from Ravi. He not even raised his head to see his dad eye to eye and did not ever utter a single word. There were tears in the poor farmer's eyes, but Ravi's eyes were not wet.

His uncle took Ravi's father out of the room and straight went to the principal's chamber. The principal could recognize the poor farmer and offered them chair. There was silence in the room. After some time Principal said "why did you never come to see how your son was doing? Why you did not see me any time".

There was no answer from Ramanna.

Then the principal said coolly and softly "Sir, unfortunately your son is in bad company. He was a good boy initially but exposure to city life had drifted him away to different path. He is into bad habits and hence his concentration was not there in studies.

He continued, this is what we see where good students fall prey to the bad way of life.

Parents should keep a vigil on their wards. We cannot do it from our side. I had warned him a couple of times but, he is out of control. He needs wise professional council.

Both brothers came out of principal's chamber dejected.

They went to the room and sat with him and never abused him but nicely counselled him. His dad though uneducated knew what may happen if he blames him or reprimands him. He put his hand on his shoulder and pulled him and hugged him. Then he said that mistakes do happen, but they could be corrected. We are with you, and nothing should deter you from going ahead.

Then they took him to their village, gave him suggestions and said that we pin lots of hope on you, and you are an intelligent student and have the capacity to improve. The first thing he said was to do away with bad elements.

Ramanna arranged professional councillors to advise Ravi.

He was taken back to his hostel, with an advice to get away from his bad friends.

Initially, it worked, and one could find changes in his behaviour. However, after couple months it was difficult for him to be away from his habits. He slowly drifted again towards his old gang.

All efforts by his dad, counsellors went in vain. His father was coming frequently to see him. He pretended to be out of old habits till he was there and back to square one after he left.

After some time Ramu learnt that his son is beyond control. He gave an ultimatum to him and said, "If you fail again, I can't send you money anymore and you may have to manage yourself". Then onwards he stopped coming to the hostel. He never expected his son to improve.

After some months came a turning point in the life of Ravi. Once they went to the city which was away from his college. They had been to the pub followed by a late-night movie. By the time they were to return it was too late. They could not dare to walk as the college was far and further, they were drunk.

They were in dilemma as to what next? In the meantime, they spotted an auto. He stopped and enquired where they wanted to go. The destination was engineering college hostel. Auto driver was conversing in fluent English and said it is dead of the night, and I can drop you, but charges will be three times the normal rate.

All the friends of Ravi had to agree as there was no alternative. As he was driving, he did enquire as to what they are studying. They all said we are in first year and we lost the term as we could not clear the exam.

Ravi asked the driver as to how come he speaks fluent English.

He replied "My dear friend, I was also a student like you in the same engineering college and got the admission on merit. My father too was an auto driver and pinned hopes on me. I lost my way and got trapped in wrong company. I did the same thing what you are doing. I failed a couple of times.

My parents could not support me financially as they had to spend money for my sister's wedding. I was distanced by my parents, and they died early may be because of my wrong doings.

In the meantime, I got married to a local girl and, I have two kids.

There was no education and hence no job for me. I followed my father's profession and diving this auto now.

As I must manage my family and pay house rent, I do extra work in the late night to earn more. He further said, "for God's sake, you don't do the mistake I did". Parents pin big hopes on us and when we turn out to be like this, they die young. He further added it is my appeal with folded hands to study well and be good Engineers. Otherwise, I am afraid you will be like me.

This touched Ravi's heart.

His dad's face came in front of him, and he saw a very sad face of him for the first time when he came to meet him after his own failure in first year BE.

Ravi took this incidence and auto driver's advice seriously. He swore on his parents in front of a Ganesh temple which he visited next day and decided to change.

He kept away from his friends and stopped his bad habits.

He concentrated on his studies totally. He was on a right track, and this truly amazed his parents. The Turing point in his life was the meeting of that auto driver and his candid advise with his personal experience.

Ravi went on clearing exams and completed his BE degree and thus Ravi's father Ramu and mother were the happiest persons and were on cloud 9 when Ravi completed his BE.

He is now a famous and most sought-after builder.

Thus, a turning point made the person forge ahead with confidence.

This may not happen all the time and many continue to be like that auto driver.

The onus is on parents to be vigilant and should keep a watch on their children and never allow them to traverse on a wrong road.

Good friends and staying focused with a dream to follow will take a person on the road to success.

ONE SHOULD ALWAYS REMEMBER THAT ONE CANNOT REACH RIGHT DESTINATION BY WALKING ON THE WRONG PATH

Forgiveness

Forgiveness isn't approving what happened. It is choosing to rise above it: Robin Sharma

To err is human, to forgive, divine: Alexander Pope

In a village, there was a family of farmers. The lady in the house was highly religious and full of common sense and lots of wisdom. She knew the mythological stories of Ramayana and Mahabharata very well. She had not only the knowledge of them but used to narrate the stories in an effective way to children not only from her house but the neighbouring houses too. She was better known in the community as "Story telling aunty." She used to involve children and made them interactive one.

With a deep interest in mythology, she named her son Dushyanta. She did not stop there and insisted (her son) Dushyanta to name his two sons as Ram and Laxman.

Both brothers grew together, and as in Ramayana, Laxman always obeyed his elder brother Ram, and his orders were "veda wakya," i.e., final verdict.

The father coming from a middle-class family, built two houses for both sons in the nearby city. But they all lived together in an ancestral house.

Both Ram and Laxman settled down well in life. Their attachment to the family made them stay together more so with mother.

Ram had a son, and Laxman had a daughter. Ram named him Vivekanand as he was impressed by the philosophy of Swami Vivekanand. Similarly, Laxman named his daughter Sarojini as Laxman had a great admiration for Sarojini Naidu.

This spiritually filled family used to follow a Guruji or a spiritual leader and attended "Satsang" or discourse.

Satsang or discourse.

They came back from Satsang with positive vibes. This led to a good attitude with positive thinking in the whole family.

Whenever Ram or Laxman used to go on business trips, they never forgot to bring gifts for both children. That was the bondage between each other.

One day, what happened was not clear, but some misunderstanding took place between both the brothers. Laxman was upset and started abusing elder brother Ram whom he had worshiped like God. He started using foul language which was a shock to Ram.

The love, faith, and affection, which was built over the years, vanished. There was no elderly person to sort out the differences as both parents had passed away. If the mother was to be alive, then such a thing would not have occurred.

Ram was very hurt. They never saw eye to eye. Even if they crossed each other anywhere, they would ignore and take a different path. Years passed and they never patched up. Ram had taken Laxman's abusive words to his heart.

Laxman's daughter's marriage was fixed. All arrangements were made. Laxman felt that something was missing. He felt that during the auspicious occasion elder brother's blessing was necessary. Finally, he decided to meet his brother and extend the invitation and seek his blessings.

Laxman and his wife went to his house and said, "Sarojini is getting married, and we all seek your blessings. I am sorry for what went wrong some years back. It was my fault; I should not have done what I did. I repented, but I had no guts to say it to you. Please forget it, pardon us, and bless our daughter".

All these pleadings made no effect on Ram. He felt that these people would never change. He had decided not to attend the wedding and did not utter a single word. Laxman returned, feeling bad.

As the family tradition goes, they were all going to Satsang of Swamiji. Laxman went to Swami to take his blessings along with his daughter. Swamiji blessed the family. However, Swamiji could notice that Laxman was not happy unlike his usual jovial mood. Swamiji asked as to why he was dull, not enthusiastic when there is a marriage in the family. Then Laman narrated the whole story and said I need my brother's blessings, which is not forthcoming.

Guruji closed his eyes, and there was a lull for some time, and he said, "God is there, believe in him."

After a few days, Ram had come for the Satsang. That time, Guruji called him and said there is a marriage in your family, and Laxman had come to give an invitation, and I learned that that you were not likely to go for the marriage. What is the matter asked the Swamiji.

Ram was upset that Laxman had informed him about it. Then he blurted out all the things that happened 20 years back. He remembered each word Laxman had spoken then.

Guruji listened to him quietly and was calm. He asked Ram that you had attended the Satsang two weeks back, a week before your brother's visit. Isn't it asked Swami. Ram nodded and said yes. Can you tell me what I had told you in that Satsang and the story which I narrated?

Ram scratched his head and could not recollect and said to Swamiji, "I am sorry that I am unable to recollect."

Swamiji said, "You have forgotten what was told a fortnight back but remember word by word what transpired 20 years back. This has not only spoiled your relationship but also snatched away your peace of mind. Carrying the dreadful things for so long is not good for health. You are an elder brother, and your name is "Ram". Learn to behave like Ram, bury the hatchet, and move on. That is life. These words of wisdom enlightened him. He thanked Swamiji, and after salutations went home happily, lessening his burden, which he was carrying for long.

He not only attended the wedding but took active part and blessed the couple wholeheartedly.

Forgiveness is an integral part of happiness.

Carrying bad thoughts and incidences or instances in mind will certainly take away peace of mind. "Forget and forgive" is the best policy to forge ahead with happiness. The state of mind should be like a clean slate without any bad scribbling which should be erased then and there. Keeping a grudge, bad opinion, and thoughts of taking revenge will not take anyone anywhere. One should remember that life is short and when there is not enough time to find a friend, why have enemies.

Learn to live happily with a clean slate, writing good memories and erasing the bad ones. This gives ultimate happiness. As Mother Terasa said “If we really want to love, we must learn how to forgive.

Loneliness is a Curse

Loneliness and feeling of being unwanted is the most terrible poverty.

-Mother Teresa

The worst thing that can happen in today's world is loneliness. In today's contemporary nuclear families, love, enjoyment, and camaraderie thrive.

In USA, well-to-do families have a big house of 4-5 bedrooms. Each child or person gets one room each. As the children grow up, they leave the house, and after retirement, they find the big house unwieldy and difficult to maintain. So, they move to smaller house after selling the old house. Not only that, but they also shift to smaller towns and ultimately to old age homes.

Whereas in our country nowadays, children go out of the house and settle down in big cities or abroad. Sometimes, they send the money back home or desert them. Unlike USA, parents have attachment towards their house, which they have built, or it is an ancestral property. They are not keen to go to old age homes as they are not comfortable, or they do not have sufficient funds to support.

Thus, the two oldies continue to stay together. The problem starts when one of them passes away. Then, loneliness looms in. It ultimately works on the mind, and they get into depression. If it is a male, he resorts to alcohol.

They find it difficult to live alone!! Loneliness is an enemy of old age. There are countries where there is a ministry for loneliness.

This is a story of an old, lonely lady.

A little boy comes from the school jumping and tells his mother that there is a different type of homework given by the teacher. Mother asks her son, "You appear to be excited, what is the homework?"

Then he says “my teacher has asked me to hug ten people and tell them to BE PATIENT, TRUST LIFE, & I LOVE YOU"

Mom told her son that today being Saturday, I am going to the mall, come with me, and you will be able to complete your homework.

The boy was super excited and got ready in the morning to go to the mall. He started his homework in the mall. By the time he had hugged nine people, his mother finished her work and told her son that it was time to go home as it was raining heavily and that he could do the last one on the way.

Her son agrees, and the car starts moving ahead. On the way, the boy spots a small house and requests her mother to stop the car, which she does as there is an ample parking place.

He knocks the door and rings the doorbell. There was no response, and he continues his effort. After some time, a grand old lady with a grim and wrinkled face opens the door to see the little boy. What is the matter? What do you want, my son? Come on in says the granny and calls him inside as it was raining.

Boy's eyes glowed and he happily said, "Can I hug you?" It was a pleasant surprise for the granny. She hugged him, and that time the boy whispered into her ears what his teacher has asked him to say." Be patient, trust life and I love you?" Hugging him tightly she asked him," tell me, who asked you to say this?

The boy said to granny, "This is my homework, and my teacher had asked me to say it to ten people, and you are the last one.

As it was quite some time, and hence boy's mother came out of the car to come inside the house and asked, "is anything wrong?"

The old lady made them sit for a while and was in tears and said, "My husband recently passed away, and there is nothing left for me in the life".

I was fed up with loneliness, so, I decided to commit suicide. I tied the rope to the roof, the stool was kept below, and a noose was to be fixed around the neck and the doorbell rang. I was wondering as to who has come as no one had dropped in anytime.

What a message he had brought "Be patient, trust life & I love you." She said Lord Jesus must have sent him with this message. Now, I decided not to go ahead with hanging myself, and I see a grandson in him. Then on the mother and her son were regular visitors and she lived happily thereafter.

Message: For older people, the combination of positive thoughts and companionship offers hope and banishes the isolating curse of loneliness.

We should appreciate teachers' thoughtfulness in shaping young minds.

Credibility makes a difference. J C Penney Store - A credible entity

All credibility, all good consciences, all evidence of truth come only from the senses.

-Friedrich Nietzsche

This is a true story during 1994-95, when I visited USA as a team leader and goodwill ambassador from India. A group study exchange team from one country to another country, stay with the family of the Rotarians in that country as it is a cultural exchange programme. My team members and I went to buy trousers from a shop in a nearby mall. While we walked out the shop, the shopkeeper kept us informed that for any reason if we did not like the product, it could be returned, and they would replace it. After returning home, I tried the trousers and the shirt and somehow felt that it was not a good product for which paid much more than it was worth. I was staying on the first floor; I came down to see the house lady who was sitting in the drawing room. I asked her opinion on my purchase, and she felt that it looked fine. However, I expressed my opinion that it was not worth that for which I paid. She said no problem, let us go tomorrow and get it exchanged if I wish to. On her enquiry when I mentioned that I had got it from the J.C. Penney store, she exclaimed my gosh! if it is from J C Penney then I can vouch for it; they will not cheat you. I always buy everything from that store. Their credibility is remarkably high. You can just be assured that you have bought the good stuff for the right price. Then I dropped the idea of going back to replace it. She further narrated the story of J C Penney. She said J C Penney chain is a large chain spread all over the US. He started with a garment store initially and he himself used to be present to supervise the things. It is said that a wealthy lady from that locality came in a Cadilac car, got down, entered the store, and said that she did not like the jacket that she had purchased from the store and would like it replaced. This practice of returning and replacing the stuff existed in the US for a long time. As J C Penney was observing the conversation, the manager was about to say something to the lady, when J C Penney intervened, took the jacket inside and asked the manager to get another stuff for the madam, whichever she likes. She took the replacement thanking Penney profusely. However, the manager was aghast, looking at J C Penney and said "Sir, the jacket she returned, is not from our store; she must have bought it from somewhere else". To that Penney said, "I do not want a client to go back unhappy. It will not make a substantial difference to me. At least, we will not lose a good client. Then onwards, the wealthy lady was a regular visitor to buy goods from J C Penney. She did realise later that she had not bought the jacket from there and greatly appreciated the thoughtfulness and kindness of Mr Penney. This was the culture which Mr J C Penney inculcated in his stores and that is how it was labelled as a credible store.

Trust is built on credibility, and credibility is earned by prioritising the needs of others before you own.

A person of integrity, credibility, gratitude, and strong character earns the affection of many and rarely faces failure.

A Rich Man's Rich Thinking

Your attitude not the aptitude will determine your altitude.

- Zig Ziglar

The true story narrated below was shared by someone on some occasion. While the name and place may not be relevant, the message is.

A rich man and his driver

A man built up his company from a scratch and went on to be a very successful person. His main purpose was to supply manpower to various institutions, corporate sectors, multinational companies and government agencies. He used to supply housekeeping staff (Safai karamchari) and other staff. His establishment grew very well and spread all over India. He also got the contract for the maintenance of the parliament. He used to move around from one place to another place to supervise the activities of the company.

He had a couple of cars and few trusted drivers too. He was addressing a conference and his thinking and action appealed to me. He said we travel in our own luxury cars and our life is in the hands of the driver. One mistake from the driver can cause calamities. Thus, I always keep a driver in whose capability, I have full faith. He should be well dressed and understand our needs too. Generally, I sit next to driver in the front seat and naturally I except him to be well mannered and well-dressed which makes us feel comfortable.

The question he asked is that we sit with the driver all the time and sometimes wake up early morning to reach the destination. It is the owner's responsibility to keep him happy. He should have good sleep, good food so that he can drive well and will not doze off. He continued and said many owners of the chauffeur driven car allow the driver to sleep in the car itself or offer a small hotel nearby which may or may not be comfortable. He said that he spends a lot of money on philanthropic work, for the education and health of many poor people. I spend a lot of money on those whom I do not know personally, then why not on my own driver who is known to me and takes care of me.

Thus, my philosophy is to keep my drivers happy and hence book a room for driver in the same hotel where I stay. It is immaterial whether it is a five star or a seven-star hotel. He also takes the breakfast in the hotel which is generally complimentary. He further said if I must leave early, I tell the hotel management to give him a wakeup and bed tea. He would never stop there but also give a ring him and say good morning and find out whether he had a good sleep. He would also instruct him that they would be leaving in next half an hour, so that he keeps the car clean and be ready to move on. Thus, I keep my drivers happy, and it is my duty to take care of them.

What a mind-set!

What an attitude!

People with big cars need to have big hearts!

A Pill to Forget My Children

The saddest of all hearts is one without gratitude: Tom Krause

There was a famous pharmacy in the heart of the city. As the business was soaring, the pharmacist had many assistants to help him in the counter. As it was across the main street, it was very easy for everyone to reach. The reputation of that pharmacy was such that even the rarest of the rare medicine were available there. When some of the medicines were not available in other pharmacy then the patients were referred to this pharmacy.

Prasad, the owner of the Pharmacy was kind-hearted and empathetic to every patient. When poor patients had no money, he would give the medicines and ask them to pay later. He was loved by all sections of society.

Right in front of his pharmacy there was a bus stop, and many people used to wait to embark on their journey. There was one lady who used to come there regularly, sit and stare at the pharmacy. She never got into any bus. It was very clear that she was not to go anywhere but certainly sitting with a purpose. The pharmacist's sharp eyes fell on this lady who was always looking at the shop for hours together. He wondered whether she wanted to buy something. One day he took the courage to go to her and said "Madam, I always see you sitting here staring at the pharmacy and you never catch a bus to go anywhere. "Do you need any medications from our pharmacy".

She said "Yes, that is the reason I come here but did not have the courage to ask you. I understand that you stock the rarest of rare medicines". Prasad said "tell me which drug you need. I shall bring it and hand over here itself". She said, "I shall tell you my son, but you come and sit next to me". He sat close to her and asked as to what she wants. She asked him if he was married, how many children he has and whether his parents are there and live with him. Prasad did not understand why she was asking these questions. Then he said "Madam, I am married, my two daughters go to school and my parents live with me. She was very happy and gave a broad smile and said how lucky you are and are fortunate to have your parents living with you son. She said, "hope you don't mind me addressing you as my son". Pharmacist Prasad said to that old lady who had wrinkles on her face and drooping shoulders, you can certainly address me as your son. Then he asked her again if she wanted any medicines. She said Oh! I have forgotten the name as my memory is failing. I will try to remember and inform you tomorrow and she left.

As usual, the very next day she again came to bus stop at the same time giving a staring look at the pharmacy. Prasad spotted her, but as he was busy, he cleared the crowd and then went and sat next to her. He asked, "do you remember the name of the tablet". She said yes, but there is a story to getting that tablet. Pharmacist said tell me what the story is.

She said, I too had a very nice family, and I was working, preparing rotis (flat breads) and supplying to vendors and my husband was an auto driver. Our aim was to see that our children get the best education like you. I too have two daughters; both were brilliant in their studies. We both worked hard day and night to save money. Fortunately, both got admission to the government engineering college. We both saved money and spent on their education.

Both have graduated and found their own partners. We had no objection. One girl is settled in Germany and other in Canada. Initially, they were visiting us once in every two years. After their father passed away none of them came for the funeral or to console me. They gave one or other excuses like they were busy in their work or with children having exams or they were on vacation etc. They had gifted me a mobile smart phone to talk to my grandchildren. Now, it is difficult for me as they talk only in English which I do not know. They have started avoiding me. They used to send money regularly but now it is almost stopped. I continue to supply rotis (flat breads) to my vendors and make my living. While narrating this life story Prasad could not miss to observe her wet eyes and eye drops trickling down. He felt so bad for the old woman as she had sacrificed so much in upbringing of her children, but she had to face such a situation in the final stages of her life. He felt that the word gratitude, responsibility and duty were missing from the dictionary of both children.

Prasad was emotionally moved and reminded her to talk about the medicine she wanted. Again, the old lady said, my son, my memory has faded away and I have forgotten the name of the medicine as I was narrating my story. I shall certainly remember it tomorrow. Prasad a humane pharmacist started thinking as to why the lady avoids naming the medicine. He imagined that probably it could be the cost of the drug. She was a lady with high self-respect and self-esteem.

Next day Prasad had decided to tell her whatever may be the cost of the medicine, he would deliver her without charging. The next day she did not come, and Prasad was disappointed and wondering as to what may have happened. However, the very next day she was spotted again. This time, Prasad left his customers and went straight to her. All of them were observing as to what he was doing and why he was looking after the old lady.

Old lady with wrinkled face appeared to be very jubilant and happily said to Prasad that she had a big order for rotis and as she could not complete it, she missed coming to bus stop the day before. She remembered her olden days again as she loved her children and with this little money, she could have purchased something for grandchildren. She remembered how she was taking children for tuitions, to participate in sports and was excited when they received prizes. When they graduated, she was on cloud 9 seeing her daughter getting gold medal. All these memories now haunt her. She has sleepless nights remembering those smiles, hugs and sweet kisses.

All these memories are good but the very thought that they will never come, never respond and even stop calling me is the one which bothers me and start thinking whether there was anything wrong in my upbringing. For both the daughters it might not matter to know whether I am alive or dead, I am sure they will not come for my final rites, and I will die like an orphan. Probably, I am fine doing something but what in store is the one that scares me. She said I want to be happy. If these memories and thoughts however sweet they may be, if they take away my happiness then the purpose of my life is lost. At that time her face became grim. She looked serious and looked into Prasad's eyes and said "my dear son, you don't to your parents what my children have done to me. You will be happy with your children and the blessings of your parents.

There are unfortunate mothers like me who suffer a lot and the dreaded thoughts of my own daughters who were given lots of love, warmth, affection and everything that was possible from our end, have distanced from me. This is not the life I wanted. Prasad too became serious and addressed her as mom and said you tell me the drug you wanted, and I will give it to you for free. She came close to him and whispered in his ears and said you store the rarest drug in your pharmacy and if you have a capsule or tablet which will erase the memory of my children, please give it. I can't live with these memories any longer which snatch my happiness. She looked into his eyes holding him tight. Prasad could see the tears continuously flowing from her eyes. She got up put her hand on Prasad's head and said, "God bless you" and she went off never to be seen again. Prasad, with deep thoughts of this old woman returned to his pharmacy with heavy heart and moistened eyes.

YOU WILL NEVER SEE A
HAPPY UNGRATEFUL PERSON

Zig Ziglar

A Big Man's Ardent Love

Attitude is a little thing that makes a big difference: Winston Churchill.

In olden days we used to get executive cars which were long and big. This is unlike the present-day cars which are high end with excellent machinery but smaller than those seen in early 50s to 70s. Those are vintage cars very rarely seen on the roads now. However, one can spot them in the old movies. There was a multimillionaire who had a couple of such cars and had drivers for them. There was one driver, who the owner liked the most because of his etiquettes, manners and humble behaviour. He always addressed the owner as 'Maalik' with folded hands and head bowed. He was the favourite of all, and this "Maalik" generally used to take him for long journeys. He was there with him for more than 25 years and nearing retirement.

He took leave to go to his native place to attend some function. It was his bad luck that he sustained a fatal heart attack in his village. His relatives informed the owner about the demise of his favourite driver. The owner was on his tour, and he clearly instructed their relatives that he would personally come and pay his last respects and attend the funeral. The family was taken by surprise that such a big man would attend the funeral of such a small man.

The owner cancelled all his engagements and asked the driver who was driving the very big car to straight away reach that village for the funeral. Not only the relatives but the whole village was waiting for this big man who was well known in the country. It was an honour for the villagers to receive such a noted personality. Many of the youngsters were went crazy looking at the big car. He got down from his car, went inside and placed the wreath on the body and talked to his wife and relatives; one could see him emotionally touched.

All preparations were made, and people were ready to carry the body. At this juncture the owner requested the body to be taken in his car even though he was aware of the ritual of family members carrying it on their shoulders. He further added that the driver was very attached to the car. Once we reach the cremation ground then you can take the body and continue with all the rituals. Everybody agreed considering this to be an honour.

As the car was very big, the body was kept on the back seat. The bigger surprise was that the owner took the keys from the driver and drove the car himself to the cremation ground. As the procession was going ahead the car was in the front and the entire village was behind the car.

This is how the big man, the owner paid his respect to his driver.

What an attitude!

What a way to offer his prayers to the departed soul!

This must have given solace to the departed soul, plenty of happiness and sense of proudness amidst sadness, to the bereaved family. May the tribe of such people increase.

IF YOU ARE GOING TO ACHIEVE EXCELLENCE IN BIG THINGS, YOU DEVELOP THE HABBIT IN

LITTLE MATTERS. EXCELLENCE IS NOT AN EXCEPTION; IT IS A PREVAILING ATTITUDE.

Collin Powell

Leave: Important in the Journey of Life

"CHANGE IS THE ONLY CONSTANT IN LIFE".

Lives of great man all remind us,
We can make our lives sublime,
And departing leave behind us
Footprints on the sands of time

Henry Wadsworth Longfellow

Life is a journey from birth to death. During this period, a human being passes through many phases. Each phase has its importance and many a time good and bad things do happen. There are good thoughts, ideas, vibes which propel one further. It is unfortunate that sometimes person clings on to the past and carries the burden to the next phase of life. It is that the bad things remain fixed rather than the good ones and that is detrimental in the next phase and is responsible for spoiling that phase.

As a person is going ahead, one must learn to leave behind memories and be ready to write on a clean slate and march ahead to make the new phase and make it enjoyable and productive. One should have a peace of mind and positive attitude. Keeping the burden of olden thoughts is the worst thing that happens and will not allow a person to move forward swiftly. Successful persons learn by their past mistakes and have a clear focus in front of them.

Let us analyse as to what a person leaves while passing from one phase of life to another till death. One must learn to leave the past and forge ahead in the present that makes one's journey a comfortable one.

It is always better to listen to the heart than the mind. Mind is a culprit and always is wavering and stores bad things easily. Mind cannot be controlled easily. If someone learns art of controlling, it then the road ahead is easy to traverse.

Heart always guides the truth and does not take one to a wrong path. That could be the reason that in our routine conversations we say heartfelt condolences, heartfelt thanks, hearty congratulations and hearty laugh.

In Hindi language we say "Dil Se." meaning from the heart.

In a comparable way we say it is my "gut feeling". Gut has nothing to do with feelings.

"If good face is a letter of recommendation, a good heart is a letter of credit."

Edward Bulwer- Lytton

"No man can feel whether he is rich or poor by turning to his ledgers. It is the heart that makes a man rich. He is rich according to what he is, not according to what he has."

Henry Waard Beecher.

Napoleon Bonaparte said 'There are two powers in this world, it is a sword and the mind. Eventually the sword is always better than the mind."

Thus, it is the mind which is a mischief monger. It is always better to control it and not allow it to control you.

BREAST ADDICTION SYNDROME

Let us begin our analysis from the very first phase after birth. The best thing that happens in this world is to have breast milk for the new-born. It is the nectar or "Amrut" and a lifeline for a baby. It is a dictum to put a baby to the breast at the earliest. We talk about rooming in or Kangaroo care (mothers' care). It is here the skin of a baby touches that of mother. In some of the western world they put the baby on to the chest of the mother as soon as the umbilical cord is cut as the caesarean section is in progress. It is said this helps a child to have bonding and they develop as strong babies and adults.

Breast fed babies gain numerous advantages due to unique qualities of breast milk that formula lacks. Babies acquire better immunity with less chances developing allergies and they grow stronger with tremendous self-confidence.

It is not surprising that our great grandmothers used to put breast milk into the infected eyes. Breast milk has lysozymes, an anti-infective agent.

It is said that breast milk may be continued until two years provided mother has sufficient milk. Nothing else other than breast milk is advised for the first six months. Depriving breast milk to a new-born is a crime. It is the legitimate right of a new-born to have exclusive breast milk for first six months unless advocated by a paediatrician.

However, baby must **leave** the breast and move on to eating habits. This is a big transition in baby's life. At times, the baby is so much attached to the breast that he or she will not leave it even when there is no milk. It becomes a habit. We call it as "Breast Addiction Syndrome ". It is worse than alcohol addiction. It is difficult to bring the baby out of it and the baby refuses to eat and ends up with problems of undernutrition.

Thus, although breast milk is the best, but a stage comes when a baby must **leave** it.

A PHASE OF SCHOOLING:

Moving on the next phase in life is schooling. It is yet another challenging phase particularly for parents.

A baby must come out of its comfort zones of family and land in a totally different atmosphere. This is not acceptable to a child. Child is for the first time taken to a Nursery class. Teacher is a stranger, other school children are new, classrooms are different. The child gets emotionally chocked, gets into anxiety and fear complex. However, parents are not aware of what is going on in that young child's mind.

The child wants to go back home and may throw temper tantrums.

The parents cannot sit around there but must leave the premises having faith on the teacher.

The child slowly comes to the terms and gets adjusted.

This is the most important phase in life wherein child learns the meaning of the word "friends". They come close and start enjoying their time with friends.

This friendship of pre-primary or primary is of paramount importance. As adults when they meet their classmates it is a nostalgic memory. That time the position one holds, the qualifications they possess never matter. Each one forgets their presence and goes back to the past and start talking in singular language. That is the intimacy of childhood friends.

Such a meeting of friends is to be experienced than talked about.

While in school one must **leave** the class as they get promoted and will miss the "miss" who taught them. At times it is difficult for some kids to get adjusted to the class teacher. However, one must **leave** those memories and go ahead.

During the education, one may have to change school or go to college after finishing the schooling. Few may go for professional colleges and few others to universities. At every step you **leave** one institution and get in to another.

Similarly, it is quite common to see change of jobs especially with IT professionals. A person needs to acclimatise in the unfamiliar environment and mingle with others, understand the principles of the management, and move on. Instead, if someone starts thinking that the previous institution or job was better and then you tend lose the opportunity to love the present job or institutions and fail to give your best.

One should always remember that yesterday was a cancelled cheque, tomorrow is a promissory note, and the present is cash in hand.

Brooding about the past and imagining tomorrow, one loses a golden opportunity to utilize the cash in hand.

One must focus on the present and concentrate on it to have better results.

Likewise, life goes on from schools to colleges to workplaces.

A YET ANOTHER IMPORTANT PHASE: THE FAMILY LIFE.

One embarks upon a new phase in life which is equally important, that is settling in life with family responsibilities.

Wedding is the most rewarding responsibility. Here, two souls meet, two strangers become very intimate in a short time. They leave the bachelorhood and move on to be a family person.

For a successful marriage there need to be a lot of give and take from both sides.

Egos, superegos, one- upmanship, authoritarian behaviour and different perspectives of life will have to be left behind if you want to sync into each other and go on smoothly. Adjustment holds the key. This leads to perfect togetherness and companionship.

When a couple celebrates their 50th or 60th wedding anniversary, it is a happy couple. When we ask them the secret of their life, majority of them have similar opinions.

They say, "I listen to her, and she listens to me". We leave our identity and our superhuman beings' nature and we work in harmony. We agree to disagree and leave that matter there itself and no more arguments. That is the beauty of togetherness. The only word that holds together is again **"leave"**. Leave your arguments, misunderstandings, forget and move on.

However, now-a-days, the marriages do not last long as it was earlier in western culture. We used to be introduced, we have three children, the first is mine (from my previous marriage), the second is my wife's (from her previous marriage) and the third is ours.

This sort of thing was never heard of in our country, but such situations are cropping up now.

Broken marriages with spouses **leaving** each other has been a trend in our society too.

Madhu was the only daughter of a construction engineer. She was very pretty and smart. She fell in love with her classmate who was tall and handsome with good physic. It was looking like a filmy couple.

They were from different casts. The proposal by Madhu to her parents to marry Sunny was summarily rejected. Parents were orthodox and it was not possible to accept it and in fact they were in shock. Finally, the mother had to give in to her daughter's demand and convinced the construction engineer to agree. Father was well to do and arranged the wedding in a massive scale as she was the only daughter even though he was not happy.

Even after two years she had not conceived, and the reason was that they did not want a baby so soon.

Then came the shocking news to Madhu's parents. Madhu said to her mother that they are divorcing. A love marriage against the wish of their parents is getting broken was not acceptable. The reason that is said to be given is that the boy was getting into cinema world and preferred to be single. What an argument or reason for divorce?

Ultimately, they had to **leave** each other and the scar on the parents was permanent and they were dejected but had to comprehend the situation.

Was the love fake? Was it just infatuation? Whether they had perfect understanding or not are the questions that come to one's mind. But this is a fact of life.

In another instance, Guru the boy and Gauri the girl was from middle class family, and both were in the engineering college. They were from the same town and classmates from school days. She was good looking but extremely ambitious. The boy was mild and simple. There was no problem in their marriage as both families were known to each other, and wedding ceremony was simple and went of smoothly.

They both got jobs in a metro town and were well settled. Gauri being cute, smart, and attractive was in the scanner of her boss. He was young and unmarried and the only son of the owner of that company. Intimacy developed which in turn developed into friendship and both started liking each other. Gauri being overly ambitious had her ulterior motives too. She knew if this marriage materializes then her fortune will open. Then the young man Surendra put this proposal to his parents. Initially they were reluctant for their son to marry a married woman. Eventually, they agreed to keep their son happy. Thus, the love marriage with a long-standing friendship came to end they had to **leave** each other. Materialistic things take over the so-called love.

There are umpteen reasons for spouses **leaving** each other even in love marriages. Unfortunately, many are for petty reasons. If a good culture is instilled in young minds and ability to judge others can be mastered and when a person has control over the mind, then arbitrations could be avoided easily.

It is equally true that there are love marriages which stood the test of time, and they continue to live happily ever and

leaving each other will never even appear in their dreams. They are tightly bound with perfect understanding and accept the fact that give and take, forget and forgive makes the togetherness strong as the days pass by.

LEAVE IN A HURRY AND REGRET FOR LIFE LONG IS THE WORST POLICY.

HAPPY LEAVING AND A SORROWFUL LEAVING.

HAPPY LEAVING

There are many instances where there is a pleasure in **leaving.** It could be when someone is going abroad for higher studies. Though it could be for some time, but it gives immense pleasure and satisfaction to everyone in the family.

In a comparable way if someone is leaving an old position or post to proceed on promotion or elevation, then certainly it is a pleasurable one.

There are no regrets whatsoever. This **leaving** has a happy ending.

SORROWFUL LEAVING

Girl gets married and after all the happy ceremonies the bride **leaves** the parents' house for ever. Father's name which was in the middle of daughter's name and the surname goes off and replaced by husband's name. Similarly, the surname which the girl was using proudly vanishes to be replaced by the surname of husband. It all happens in a fraction of a second after marriage.

When the bride is finally **leaving** her own house, it a truly a sorrowful bidding or leaving.

Similarly, when a son tells his father that he is going to leave and set up his own house separately is again a sorrowful bidding. Parents may not like it but must listen to and honour their son's decision. This is very painful and though the parents may not express it overtly and suffer silently.

Thus, there are many occasions in life where in **leaving** will leave a vacuum and bitter taste.

THREE PHASES OF ADULT LIFE

First 15 years of wedded life is at its best in togetherness. The life is fully colourful right from the days of honeymoon. Life is full of merriment, lovely and with all cheers. here is no scope for misunderstanding. This is the time when the young ones are gifted by nice kids or at times only one kid. The couple is on cloud nine.

The next 25 years are different. They are quite busy in their professions and vocations and a lot of work pressure; more responsibilities leave a husband with less time towards household activities. Profession is naturally a priority.

Similarly, if the spouse is a working woman, then it becomes too difficult to balance between family and work.

Beautiful wife is no more beautiful in the eyes of husband. Wife is not so worried to keep herself looking great as she is busy with household work and children. In the busy schedule of both spouses, sex takes a back seat. Outdoor visits or outings lessen. Misunderstanding and difference of opinions crop up and, they both continue to travel on parallel roads. There is chance of fighting for small or silly reasons.

HOUSEWIFE / HOMEMAKER

Even a non-working lady has a busy schedule. It is wrong to say that a wife is 'just a housewife' in fact. she is a homemaker.

One day, old classmates met each other after a long time. Ramesh was working in a multinational company, and his wife was not in any job. His friend Suresh and his wife Suma were bankers and were in high positions.

They met in Ramesh's house for dinner. Sujata, the spouse of Ramesh had prepared an excellent tasty dinner. She was the only nonworking women amongst the four. Suresh complimented her for the preparations. Ramesh said after all she is a housewife and learnt cooking from her mother. Suresh got upset with the word " She is housewife". Even Suma got offended and belittled.

Then, being a good friend, Suresh said to Ramesh that he has some questions to ask. Ramesh said' 'go ahead'.

Suresh: Who gives bath to your both kids?

Ramesh; My wife

Suresh: Who takes them to school?

Ramesh: My wife, of course

Suresh: who looks after the kids' homework?

Ramesh: My wife, she is good at it.

Suresh: Who goes shopping?

Ramesh: she, where do I have the time?

Suresh: Who pays for all household things like electricity bill, milk man, etc.

Ramesh: Where is the time for me to do all these?

Suresh: Do you help in the cooking?

Ramesh: I do not know ABC of cooking. Even she prepares a cup of tea when I come back from office.

Then Suresh started his sermon and said she is the lady behind the running of the whole house. She manages it all alone. She is working more than you. She is a homemaker and not just a housewife. He vehemently said we need to change the nomenclature. This housewife word should be deleted from the dictionary. A lady is the embodiment of peace and tranquillity in the house. With all this, Ramesh's attitude changed. It was a joyful day for Suma for being complimented adequately.

This should be a lesson to everyone in every family to respect a mother who holds the key to happiness. It is high time to leave the olden word " housewife" and make a new beginning for the women empowerment.

THE LAST PHASE; OLD AGE

This is a special phase where in there is excitement of phase one of early life and of 15 years of married life. It is the time one does not leave the other even for a short time. It is smooth sailing. It is a stage of cool life with better understanding and no ups and downs. There is no question of leaving each other but a time to hold on. If the word **leave** comes, it is when one must **leave** this world. It is time to retrospect the best time spent together, and the excellent memories harboured so long.

It is difficult to leave the company of life partners who supported each other in all ups and downs of the journey of life.

However, **leaving** is inevitable and one must accept the reality of life.

A RETIRED JUDGE AND HIS WIFE.

Here are some examples of how life partners bid farewell to the beloved and their sentiments.

Anant Kumar was a leading advocate and later took over as a Judge. He has passed many (landmark) judgements of high order. After retirement, he went in for social service and was continually active in it. He and his wife Mandakini were spotted at every social event where in poor people were taken care of. They were the most adored couple and never missed attending any wedding ceremonies and other social events.

It was unfortunate that Mandakini passed away after a brief illness ending their 48 years of togetherness.

Many prominent people including politicians, Mayor, Judges, advocates, and friends came to pay their last respect.

Before the final journey, Anant Kumar thanked everyone for their condolences. He said "I know I lost a gem of a person, but I know this is not in our hands. I also know that I will miss her for ever, but she had a peaceful death without any sufferings. She was loved and respected by all. Destiny of a person cannot be changed, I will have to learn to live alone and confident of living with zeal and enthusiasm with her fond memories and your support". I am grateful for your visit, words of sympathy and your heartfelt condolences. With folded hands he thanked everyone.

This was a cool well composed senior person with perfect attitude. Even though his long-term life partner left him, he took it in right spirit. A lesson to be learnt.

GOLDEN JUBILEE OF WEDDING

Rahesh and Sudharani were a happy go lucky couple. They had two sons, a daughter, two daughters in law and a son in law with six grandchildren. A genuinely happy family. This couple had no illnesses whatsoever and used to travel a lot and spend enjoyable time with grandchildren.

The family decided to celebrate this 50th Wedding Anniversary on a large scale. All the relatives from far and near attended the Golden Jubilee wedding anniversary and greeted the couple. There was music, dance, and merriment. Even Rajesh and Sudharani enjoyed dancing. It was a day to be remembered by everyone.

The very next day, there was a great shock to everyone in the house.

Sudharani had a heart attack and died.

A home which was full of happiness and merriment turned into a home of sadness and shock.

No one could believe it, but that was the truth. Every eye was wet and few were sobbing. Dead silence cropped in. It was difficult for anyone to console the old man. He was sitting on a chair in a corner with closed eyes with folded hands not able to believe what had happened.

The body was shifted to funeral ground for final rights. Everyone talked about Sudharani and remembered their connections and what a nice lady she was. Generally, closest relatives refrain from talking as they are emotionally chocked. However, Rajesh could say that Sudha has left a void and vacuum in his life. What a day she has chosen to leave this world! She has chosen a day where in all the relatives are there to bid goodbye to leave this world to attain Moksha. If it were on some other day some of you would not have come. She left this world with fond memories. Only a lucky person gets this opportunity to leave this world like this. He further stated that he appreciates everyone's presence in this last journey of her life.

Rajesh showed a lot of thoughtfulness and tranquillity of mind to keep the emotions under control and be calm.

A PAINFUL LEAVING, LEAVING A SCAR.

Pashupati and Renuka's wedding were an arranged one. They were a made for each other couple. They had a daughter and named her Trupti. When their friends asked them why they named the very first child Trupti, they were clear in their mind and said we are satisfied with one child. She is my daughter as well as son, and we don't want any more children, so we have named her Trupti.

They had brought her up with lots of love and affection. Pashupati was a big-time contractor and built many magnificent buildings and bridges etc. He was well known and well connected.

After Trupti's graduation, her marriage was fixed. The bride groom was from a well to do family and his father too was a big-time contractor at Bangalore.

The wedding was in a massive scale and with all pomp and grandeur. You name a person of prominence of a city, they were there. With the excellent connectivity from both sides there were ministers, MLAs, and all who is who in the city were there to greet the couple.

After the wedding, the bridegroom party were ready to leave for Bangalore. The convey of cars was lined up. Renuka the bride's mother accompanied her daughter.

Trupti hugged her father, and it was an emotional bidding. It was a great wedding and perfect in order. Once they reached the bridegroom's home, all formalities were completed.

The very next day, Renuka left Bangalore, blessing her daughter as she left her new home. She wished her all the happiness and left in a car along with the driver.

It is said "All is well that ends well".

But in this case, it was not to be so. As she was travelling back home, Renuka met with a nasty accident. It was a head on collision, and she died on the spot.

After the postmortem, the body was brought home. Trupti along with her relatives rushed back with profound grief. It was the greatest shock of his life for Pashupati. He lost his consciousness and had to be addressed by the doctor. The sadness spread over to everyone at home and in the city as they had witnessed the happy moments during the wedding.

Pashupati took a long time to recover but the life was not the same thereafter.

Thus, a spouse who leaves the world suddenly, unexpectedly leaves a big scar and more so for the living spouse. It was a painful and bitter **leaving** and in such situations the happiness is snatched away suddenly and makes it difficult to come to terms. Time is the only healer, and it was to be for Pashupati and his near and dear ones.

When a family member **leaves** this world, it certainly has an impact on the minds of ones left behind. It all depends how one **leaves**, at what age and the way of how they leave also matters. Everyone in the planet knows that no one is eternal but still in reality one lives like they are eternal. Then, when the time to leave comes it is difficult for anyone to accept but one must accept the reality and move on. World never stops anywhere, and a human must compromise and learn to move on with fine memories and erasing the bad ones. That is life.

Life is a journey and like in any journey people come into our lives and leave at the station where they are destined to disembark. The journey continues with people on board till someone else leaves the journey. This is a life cycle for everyone in this world irrespective of what money they have or what position they have held. We are all temporary and if we understand this philosophy of life, the behaviour and attitude of every person will change towards it. Such persons are loved and liked by everyone.

"LIFE IS SHORT, THE VANITIES OF LIFE ARE TRANSIENT AND THOSE ALONE LIVE WHO LIVE FOR OTHERS AND REST OF THEM ARE MORE DEAD THAN ALIVE."

Swami Vivekananda

The Final Sacrifice

We are at our best when we give the ultimate sacrifice of putting other people, putting the country, putting our communities ahead of ourselves.

Cory Booker

Twenty years ago, a letter from a village in Himachal Pradesh, arrived at the Ministry of Defence. The writer was a schoolteacher, and his request was as follows:

He asked, "If possible, could my wife and I be granted the permission to see the place where our only Army son died a heroic death in the Kargil war, on the day of his first death Anniversary, on 07/07/2000? It's okay if you can't, if it is against national security, in which case I will withdraw my application".

The Department Officer who read the letter, said, "It does not matter what the cost of their visit is, I will pay it from my salary, if the department is unwilling to and I will bring the teacher and his wife to the place where their only son died" and he issued an order.

On the Remembrance Day of the deceased hero, the elderly couple were brought to the ridge with due respect. When he was taken to the place where his son died, everyone on duty stood erect and saluted. But one soldier, handed him a bunch of flowers, bowed and touched his feet and wiped his eyes and saluted.

The teacher said, "You're a Soldier - Why do you touch my feet?"

"Well, sir", said the soldier "I am the only one here who was with your son and the only one here who saw your son's heroism on the field. The enemies were shooting hundreds of bullets per minute with their H.M.G. Five of us advanced to thirty feet and we were hiding behind a rock. I said, 'Sir, I am going for the 'Death Charge'. I am going to take their Bullets and run to their bunker and throw the grenade. After that you all can capture their bunker.' I was about to run towards their bunker, but your son said, "Are you crazy? You have a wife and children. I am still unmarried, I will go, do the Death Charge and you Do the Covering". Without hesitating, he snatched the grenade from me and ran into the death charge.

Bullets fell like rain from the enemy's A.M.G. Your son dodged them, reached the enemy bunker, took the pin out of the grenade, and threw it right into the bunker, sending thirteen enemies to their death. Their assault was over, and the area came under our control. I lifted your son's body, sir. He had forty-two bullets in him. I lifted his head in my hands and with his last breath he said, "Jai Hind!"

I asked the superior to give permission to bring his coffin to your village, but he refused.

Though I never had the privilege of putting these flowers at his feet, I have the privilege of putting them at yours, "sir."

The teacher's wife was crying softly into the corner of her pallu, but the teacher did not cry.

The father said, “I bought a shirt for my son to wear when he would come on leave, but he never came home, and he never will. So, I brought it to put it where he died. Why don't you take it and wear it for him, beta”?

The Kargil hero's name was Captain Vikram Batra.

His father's name is Girdhari Lal Batra.

His mother’s name is Kamal Kanta.

These are our real heroes. Supreme sacrifices cannot be compared with any other sacrifices.

Children's Mind is Like a Sponge.

NEVER INSTIL A BAD THOUGHT OR WORRISOME INSTANCES.

PUNISHMENTS CAN'T REPLACE DISCIPLINE.

"In the little world in which children have their existence, whosoever brings them up, there is nothing so finely perceived and so finely felt as injustice."

Charles Dickens

Too often we forget that discipline really means to teach, not to punish. A disciple is a student, not a recipient of behavioural consequences. Our dreams and stories may contain implicit aspects of our lives even without our awareness.

Dr Dan Siegel

Children are gift of God. They are innocent and they grasp good or bad things fast. Anything taught during this younger age remains for life. It has repercussions during adult life.

So, parents and teachers need to be careful in dealing with a child when they are in pre-primary or primary school or in that age group.

CELEBRITY'S DEPRESSION

There was a celebrity who was going in for depressions often. She confessed and revealed it in public that she could link it to her childhood scare.

Without any hesitation she revealed being a victim of sexual abuse during her childhood from a close relative and that was haunting her all the time even in her adulthood. Despite trying to erase it, the thought stuck to her mind so badly that it troubled her most of the time. That is the repercussion of a bad memory of the childhood.

FEAR OF DARKNESS (Nyctophobia)

Similarly, there was a lady who was very scared of darkness. She was afraid of going alone in a dark room including the bathroom. Even in her adulthood she never stepped into the first floor of her house alone. She always needed company. The reason for that again traced back to her childhood. Her parents used to put her in a dark room as a part of punishment. At times the door was not opened till the next day. That was a harsh punishment to a child.

That was too scary, and she used to weep and go to sleep without food. A bad way of punishment for a child. I would say it is criminal. This remained fixed in her mind lifelong.

FEAR OF WATER (Aquaphobia)

In another instance a lady a fear of water. She never stepped in any swimming pool. Despite her classmate's insistence or persuasion, she did not dare to put her leg into the swimming pool. The reason was she was taken by her parents on a holiday to a resort along with other family members. She was very small, and all the kids were taken to a swimming pool. She was given an inflatable swimming ring. She was moving in the swimming pool and enjoying it. Her peers who were smaller were also swimming. As she was in the middle of the pool, she slipped from that swimming ring and started drowning. It was unfortunately not noticed by anyone. When her cousin who was much older than her spotted that the girl was missing, he immediately went nearer the place where she was swimming and found that she was drowning.

He screamed and pulled her out. There was a doctor in the family who gave her mouth-to-mouth respiration and chest compressions, and a lot of water came out of her mouth. With his timely help she survived. This impacted her a great deal and she feared water from that day and never ventured into the water even in the company her friends or relatives.

Thus, any bad incidence or instance in the early childhood would have a long-lasting impact on a child's mind.

Similarly, any punishment to a child whether at home or at school will leave a scar on the young mind of a child.

A TEACHER'S SEVERE PUNISHMENT TO A 2ND STANDARD CHILD.

I am a paediatrician and once a father brought his son studying in 2nd standard with the complaint of severe pain in the lower limbs and weakness and rundown condition. As a doctor these types of symptoms give us a thought of neurological conditions or dengue fever or viral myalgia's i.e., muscular pains. Examination did not reveal anything significant. I further probed and asked whether he was perfect in his health the previous day. Father said he was normal but started having these complaints after coming from the school. Then I further probed as to anything that happened during the school. Father was quiet for some time. When I said, "tell me sir, if anything had happened in the school?"

He then said that his son had punishment in the school as he had not done the homework. The teacher had asked him to have ten rounds of the ground. It was a big playground, and the poor kid did it but could not complete even six rounds and fell. Further, he was asked to stand in the classroom. This is the reason he had pain in the limbs, and he is feeling very weak, the father said.

I was furious at the kind of punishment and is which is against the law. I asked that teacher's name and that of the school. The father said" Why sir? I told him that I know the Commissioner of Public Instruction personally and I shall inform him and lodge a complaint. The father meekly said 'doctor if you do that, the teacher may lose his job. I don't want that to happen. I had approached him, and he regretted his behaviour and said sorry. Further he added "I know the teacher and he is from a poor background and must support his parents. Let us leave at that. "

This was the concern of that noble father who was soft on that teacher despite the severe punishment to his son.

Punishments of this type are condemnable and wrong in the eyes of law. Secondly, they would have a damaging impact on the child's mind. Teachers should understand this aspect and never give any corporal punishments to any child. Discipline and corrections can be brought in by various other means. Present day teachers are to be polished and sophisticated in dealing with kids remembering that they have a delicate mind.

CHILD STEALS FROM SCHOOL.

Raju was a first standard student. He was the son of an executive in a corporate sector and his mother was a social worker. Raju was a go getter and friendly with everyone and a pet student of his teacher. He was loved by parents for being the only son.

One day Raju came jumping and was in a happy mood. As he entered his home his mother asked him "what is that makes you so happy today? Did you get praise from your teacher?"

Raju proudly said, "Do you know mom, I got four pencils from my classmate Pooja's school bag?"

She did not know that I have picked it from her school bag. Look, these are the four, he showed it to his mom. She got disturbed and said " You thief, I never knew you could do this and hit him on his head. This was the first time he got such a scolding and a beating. Raju too was shocked as he never expected this reaction from his mom. Further, his mother told him that she would let his father know about what he had done. He will punish you hard. You bring shame to us, you nasty boy!!

Raju did not understand what was going on; for him it was a heroic act of getting pencils from Pooja's box without her knowledge. He was after all just a six-year-old kid. However, he knew something has gone wrong and what he did may not be correct.

His mother did not talk to him for the entire day till her husband came from the office. Raju, a jumping Jack was feeling uncomfortable and was wondering, as to what is in store after dad's return from office. He was expecting harsh treatment from his dad. All this was working on his mind.

This is the first time he got the punishment in his life in the form of beating and harsh words.

He was distressed and depressed as his heroic act went in vain.

The whole evening went like as if days have passed for little Raju.

Finally, dad's car arrived and the customary honking to inform his arrival. This boy who used to jump and hug his dad remained silent and almost hid himself away.

Dad walks in and says, " Where is Raju, he didn't come to welcome me!"

Mom said, “do you know what your son has done today in the school?"

What happened? Dad was curious to know. Then she went inside and dragged Raju from where he was hiding and made him stand in front of dad the executive who came with his full suit and tie. This little fellow was trembling in his half pant and waiting to see what the punishment in store was.

However, dad was cool and when he understood that Raju had stolen four pencils, he just lifted Raju, kissed him on the cheeks, and said “baby don't do these things. It is not right and next time you are not going to do this "and got a promise from Raju. This was a great surprise to Raju. Dad did not stop at that and said further “if you want pencils let me know, I can get dozens from my office."

OMG!! A bigger thief!!!

Here two things are to be noticed.

One is that the child never felt what he did was wrong and it amounts to theft. For him it was a heroic act. She should have counselled him instead of punishing. She should not have scared him of punishment by his father.

It is unfortunate that in many homes father is depicted as villain and all punishments are rooted through him. Unfortunately, fathers must withstand the most of correcting their children.

Parents need to be cautious in implementing punishments to children. Wise counsel is the best art which every parent should learn. Punishments of any kind will in fact be detrimental to a child. It may so happen that this will remain in their delicate mind for a long time.

The father telling the son that he can bring more pencils from office is not in good taste and little older child can understand that he is stealing from his office.

Children look to their parents as role models, and they need to keep up the standards.

Parenting is an art. It is not taught anywhere and hence parents need to be vigilant in their behaviour.

At no cost one should bring turmoil in the young minds by parents' action.

GRAND FATHER PUNISHES GRAND SON.

Punishments by grandparents to their grandchildren are a rare phenomenon. All grandparents give unconditional love, time, and energy to the grand kids. As a parent one finds it difficult to devote time due to their work pressure and that is the time when they are all building their carriers. Whereas grandparents have plenty of time to offer to the grandchildren. They enjoy the time spent with kids and children love it and reciprocate it.

Whenever parents punish their kids they straight away run to the grandparents for solace & they get it too. The soft corner by grandparents sometimes is the cause of disagreement between parents and grandparents. We often hear parents telling "you are spoiling our kids because of your extreme love."

Grandparents are tempted to offer chocolates, ice-creams, and even junk food even without the knowledge of the parents. Whether it is right or wrong is a different issue.

As a paediatrician myself, I am against any punishments to children. Mistakes are bound to happen but to give severe punishments like slapping, beating, abusing, making them stand outside the house in sun, locking in a dark room etc are uncalled for. The age difference between a child and a parent is generally more than 20 years. What is the greatness in showing one's power by hitting a small child who has no way to protest or protect himself. It is criminal. The impact on a child is tremendous as child cannot express himself.

Children growing up in an environment where there are regular punishments would end up with a personality of a rebel and never be peaceful but certainly be an agitated adult.

I never gave such type of punishments at any time to my children and saw that no one else punishes them for whatever reason. Ours is a "no punishment home."

However, we resorted to nice counselling and at times different modes.

Once, I vividly remember that my son got an ice candy with a stick. Those days sellers used to bring them in a box on a bicycle. They used to shout at a high pitch "Ice cream, Ice cream, (though it was ice cream, but those guys pronounced it differently). They shouted at the top of their voice to reach out to kids and attract them. We never gave our children that stuff any time.

One day my son got such an ice cream from a family friend and was happily enjoying it. For his misfortune, I saw him. Looking at me he tried to hide it and was nervous. He was expecting a scolding from me. I was calm and snatched that red ice cream on a stick which was half eaten and pulled it from that stick on my palm and smeared it on his face. He did not cry as he knew that it was his mistake. Everyone in the house saw it. Then onwards he never touched the ice cream.

As any grandfather and a firm believer on no punishments, I never punished or scolded my grandchildren. When I have not punished my own children how can I punish my grandchild?

However, one day I committed a grave mistake. Small kids are in the habit of getting the mobile phones from their parents. As they do not give it easily then the soft targets are grandparents.

Thus, my grandson Aarav used to get my mobile and play some games. My mobile was full of his apps. He was just four years old. I changed my mobile and got a brand new costly one. My wife said do not give this one to kids and also warned them not to touch my mobile. I went to my bedroom on the first floor and Aarav followed me. I was in the dressing room adjacent to the bedroom where there is a table and chair where I usually write my books. He with a small face said "Baba, will you give your mobile for some time?" I took pity on him and as a typical grandfather and said not to tell his grandmother, hold it with both hands firmly, go and sit on my bed and play his games. "This is a new costly one that I purchased today". He jumped in joy as he was not expecting me to give it to him. He took the mobile and holding with both his hands as advised went jumping to the bedroom.

Suddenly, I heard a loud "thud". I ran to see what had happened. My mobile was on the floor on the other side of the bed and this boy was standing on another side. I went to see whether there was a crack on the glass or any other damage. I straight away came and firmly slapped on his cheek and shouted at him saying " You idiot, I had told you to hold it tight and go to bed. Why did you throw it?". He did not cry but putting his head down in shame said " Baba, I threw it on the bed and wanted it to land on the bed but unfortunately it landed on the other side of it on the floor. "

This landing of the mobile amazed me. I felt I should not have slapped him in a fit of rage. I pulled him and hugged him said " it is OK baby, but I should not have slapped you. Will you please forgive me?" I kissed him firmly and said sorry couple of times.

He was calm and asked me "Baba, what is the meaning of Idiot?" I had abused him with the word idiot.

Further, he asked me not to tell anyone in the house and especially the grandmother. I never mentioned this to anybody for a month and casually talked about if one day when everything was cool.

I feel, there is nothing wrong in saying sorry to a small boy. Irrespective of the age or position you hold there is nothing wrong in apologising if you were wrong. The lesson that I learnt is to never act in anger and learn to be calm.

That was my first and the last punishment to my grandchildren. I feel sorry about it even now. Hopefully, the young lad will not carry it in his mind.

Mistakes happen and they could be corrected. However, it is apt to have a control over the mind and never overreact. Learn to be cool.

Thus, we see children getting punishments at home or schools and at times they are harsh. Its repercussions are bad it could last long. Children may not express it, but it is hidden in their mind. It may change his or her personality depending on the type of punishments and how often.

Discipline is necessary for any errant child but one should remember **"punishments can never replace discipline".** Parents should learn the art of disciplining their children and not use their authority as weapon on small kids.

Teachers should be aware that corporal punishments are against the law. Because of fear, children generally refrain from bringing it to the notice of parents. Many times, they suffer internally.

It is surprising to note that these punishments still exist in many schools, both government and private. It is the same story whether in a village school and in the posh urban school. As a paediatrician I coax and ask my patients whether they get any punishment in the school. The first reaction is "no." When I further coax and ask them what teachers do when you misbehave or make a mischief. For that they say "yes, for that we get punishments." Every child for that matter receives punishments. It may be small or big, but the favourite punishment of teachers is to hit a child on their hands or the back, by their own hands or with a cane.

We need to change. Teachers are never told how to punish a child in their curriculum. For parents, there is no school to learn about good parenting. Thus, these mistakes happen, and I am afraid, they may continue to happen.

FRAGILE CHILDREN MUST NEVER BE PUNISHED HARSHLY.

THERE ARE UMPTEEN WAYS OF CORRECTIONS.

Let us not snatch away their childhood by our way of disciplining them.

CHILDREN NEED LOVE, ESPECIALLY WHEN THEY DO NOT DESERVE IT

Harold Hulburt

I MAY NOT BE ABLE TO GIVE MY KIDS EVERYTHING THEY WANT, BUT I GIVE THAT WHAT THEY NEED: LOVE, TIME, ATTENTION, YOU CAN'T BUY THESE THINGS

Nishan Panwar

Challenged Children Are Second to None

One who fears failure limits his activities. Failure is simply an opportunity to begin again, this time more intelligently: Henry Ford

Group Study Exchange Program of Rotary International is truly a learning experience.

GSE was a flagship program of Rotary in the past which is now converted to VTT (Vocational Team Training).

I was fortunate to be the leader of such a team of four young non-Rotarian professionals. They were Economist, Psychiatrist, medical doctor, and a lady Architect.

The beauty of the program was that we stay with hosts and not in hotels and it is a reciprocal program.

We were taken to schools, colleges, universities, Courts and even Governor's office.

The purpose of the cultural exchange was to understand the various cultures of those countries interacting with varieties of people across different vocations.

I was taken to a challenged children's school where in they used to pick up talents and interests in those children.

This was back in 1995, and I was amazed to see the challenged children managing the computers. In those days we never had computers in our schools.

As I was observing a kid from the back, he noticed me and said, “Good morning, sir.” It was a pleasant surprise to me as I never expected that courtesy from him.

The guy who was with me introduced him as "he is a mentally retarded trying his hand on computers.”

The boy got wild and said, “I am not mentally retarded; I am a slow learner." I am good at computers. He was upset as that sentence hurt him. His ego was touched. What I appreciated is the presence of mind of that child and the way he came out to defend himself, that showed how he cared for his self-esteem. Certainly, such children will do well as they grow.

The guy who introduced the child apologized to him. Yet another decent quality of elderly.

I told the child how much I was impressed by looking at him using the computer.

In our country, children are not fortunate to own computers. On that remark the boy said I do hope children in your country too will get computers soon and they too enjoy like me. What a mature statement from a challenged child!!

Now, our children have the computers and enjoy using it.

All challenged kids also should get into the learning the art of Computers and get the best opportunity.

What impressed me is the high self-esteem of that challenged child and his confidence. He felt that he is second to none.

That was a great learning experience for me.

NO JOB IS SMALL: Ice cream selling boy's self-confidence!!

It is seen that in US that children are allowed to do petty jobs to earn money. Even children of ultra-rich parents go for small jobs. This is to teach the ground realities of life, earn a bit of money with hard-work and develop a habit of saving.

I was staying with a host in USA during Group Study Exchange Program.

As he was explaining their lifestyles, I too explained about our traditions and lifestyles. I had taken albums of weddings, thread ceremonies, festivals like Holi, Diwali (festival of lights), our Temples, Churches, and other places of worship. I did explain the importance of Sapta Pati, Mangal sutra in weddings and why we play colours and significance of aarti, and Tulsi plant in front of the house and many more. Americans are aghast when we reason out the significance of our festivals.

In continuance of their practices and culture the host who was very well to do and well placed, took me to a small street where he said that he was distributing the newspapers in his childhood.

He further said he enjoyed doing it and saved some money too. I asked him why he did it and sent his children for petty jobs when he had lots of money. He said it is a good culture in our society. Everybody does it. Even Presidents of USA did it in their childhood.

The purpose is to understand the value of money, hard work, importance of savings, to learn interpersonal relationships and communication skills. It has a profound impact on the young minds he said.

Further he said that kids work in restaurants, petrol stations, ice cream parlours, few joints like

MacDonald's etc.

One day I went to an ice cream parlour, and I saw a young boy at the counter selling ice creams. He greeted me saying: Good morning, sir, we have so many flavours, choose one.

I picked up one and said this is my choice. The young lad looked into my eyes and with a smile said, "What a perfect Choice!!" This is my choice too.

To that I said " You are a clever boy and must be telling the same thing to everyone irrespective of what their choose is.

The boy said" Sir, I am honestly telling you what I like. I am not a businessperson but just a seller, and he added "I still say that you picked up my choice."

That was the clarity, clear thoughts, and boldness in that boy, which I liked.

They learn to be impressive, learn perfect communication, and art of expressiveness.

This I believe it to be a nice culture. Even kids of rich people learn to be humble and learn dignity of labour. In India many of the children of rich people are spoilt sport and it is because of their father's money and position.

It is a beautiful culture to understand that "NO JOB IS SMALL"

One should learn to respect all professions and vocations irrespective of the nature of work.

Self-Esteem; Self-Confidence; I Can Do 'Spirit'

Key component for youngsters

STORY OF CHICK & EAGLET

An eagle by mistake laid its egg in a tree nearby a poultry. The egg hatched and a baby eaglet came out of it.

As it jumped out of the tree, it could see plenty of chicks moving around and it joined the group, spending fun time with them all. They were of the same age.

Eaglet used to jump like chicks taking few steps and hopping from one end to a another with small jumps like the other chicks. It was enjoying the company and was comfortable.

It so happened that one day an older motherly eagle could see the eaglet from the sky and started wondering why the eaglet is mingling with those chicks and just hopping like them. It was annoyed and next day it decided to teach the eaglet a lesson.

On the next day, the big eagle flew down from the sky straight to the poultry where the eaglet was with chicks.

As if it was diving down, came directly to the eaglet, and picked it up went high into the sky. The eaglet was wondering as to what was going on. As the mother eagle reached a great height, it just dropped the eaglet. It could have been a shock of its life. As it was coming down sharply, it had no other choice than to beat its feathers forcefully. It was the question of survival.

Guess what? Something amazing happened. It started flying on its own beating the feathers. The eaglet understood its strength and really enjoyed flying high in the sky. Hitherto, it never understood its innate capacity and feeling that it could only jump like chicks.

So, every human being, more so children, underestimate themselves and never realize their innate capacities or potentials and they are extremely comfortable in their comfort zones. Everybody has an innate capacity, but self-esteem should be energized and open their wings to have self-confidence.

One needs to take a bit of risk and accept the challenge to be successful. One should inculcate "I can do spirit "in themselves to forge ahead.

If you do not do it then you remain like an eaglet without knowing its own capabilities.

In life, one should never remain like chick but fly high in the sky much above the other birds to reach the pinnacle of success.

It is the responsibility of parents and teachers to identify the potentials of the kids and add wings to fly to realise their dreams.

Amazing Ugandan Experience

Success is not final; failure is not fatal:
It is the courage to continue that counts.

Winston Churchill

Reaching out to the poor is the motto of social organizations, including Rotary. These philanthropic activities are done in our own country. An opportunity came my way to serve beyond borders. It was Intercontinental Medicare Project of Rotary International to service poor in East Africa.

I led the team of eleven South Indian doctors to Uganda. We performed our operations at Iganga and Maska hospitals. We had experienced doctors in most of specialties. We were amazed to see the poverty in those places, which was beyond our imagination.

Our team examined 3956 patients and operated on 833 patients successfully. We performed intricate operations and would like to highlight two tricky situations which we encountered.

Indian doctors save the life of a young lady.

There were three operating tables, three surgeons operated simultaneously, and the only anaesthesiologist was hopping from one table to another.

As it was a referral hospital, there was one more operation theatre.

Once there was commotion; nurses and ward boys were moving helter-skelter. I asked the nurse as to what the matter was.

The surgeon there opened the abdomen and failed to find the reason for bleeding, and the patient was in shock. I summoned our surgeon and anaesthetist, and they jumped into action.

It was a case of ruptured tubal pregnancy. They completed the surgery in no time and managed the shock and gave a lease of life. She would have otherwise gone.

Her name was Lima Teddy, 25 years old, and was in deep trouble. It was the swift action of our team that saved her life. All the doctors and nurses praised our excellent Indian team.

The image of our doctors was further elevated in the hospital and in the whole city by word of mouth. Lema Teddy recovered before our camp was over and thanked us profusely and was very emotional.

That was the competency of our Indian doctors.

BELIEVE IN YOURSELF! HAVE FAITH IN YOUR ABILITY!

WITHOUT A HUMBLE BUT REASONABLE CONFIDENCE IN YOUR

OWN POWERS YOU CANNOT BE SUCCESSFUL OR HAPPY.

- Norman Vincent Peale

The Lady Who Made Us Shiver

In the camp there came a hefty lady weighing around 110 kg. She had a huge thyroid swelling around the neck. Our surgeons looked at the lady and decided to remove the thyroid swelling. I was worried as a leader of the team because of its size. I told the surgeon that it is too huge to be operated in a camp like this. However, a competent surgeon was confident that he would be able to do it. Hesitantly, I gave the go ahead but asked them to be careful as no major surgeries were performed in the hospital for a long time although it was a referral hospital. It was difficult to arrange blood too. There were many constraints.

That lady was so obese that it was difficult to put her on the operating table. Half of her body was out of the table because of her girth!

A major portion of the huge thyroid tumour was almost removed, but in the meantime, she turned blue.

Anaesthesiologist immediately brought the jumbo oxygen cylinder and opened, and to his surprise it was empty. We were shown all the requirements by locals before starting the camp. However, we assumed that the oxygen cylinder would be full.

More than the surgeon or anaesthesiologist, I was shivering in my pants as it was my responsibility as the leader. If she had died, it would have brought a bad name to the country, and we had to face all the consequences. All these thoughts passed through my mind. However, the surgeon was very cool. He pulled out the huge thyroid immediately and saw the pressure on windpipes was released, and she turned pink. The crisis was over, and she was shifted to post-operative ward.

Believe me; I could not sleep that night. I only prayed for her recovery.

I saw her the next morning, going first to her. She was awake and gave a big smile, pointing to her neck that the swelling had gone. I thanked God profusely.

Even now, when I imagine that moment, I get shivers down my spine.

That was the competency of our efficient surgeons who managed the tricky situations very efficiently.

At the end of the camp, the Union Minister for health, the Government of Uganda, and Deepak Rai, the high Commissioner to Uganda praised Indian doctors and thanked for the successful camp. It hit the headlines of all local daily newspapers.

CHAPTER II

GOD DOES EXIST

God Does Exist

A WELL-KNOWN CARDIAC SURGEON WHO DID NOT BELIEVE IN GOD

Believe in your heart that you're meant to live a life full of passion, purpose, magic and miracles.

- Roy J Bennett

In this world there are plenty of people who strongly believe in God, their day will not start without salutation and prayers to God. Few of them never fail to visit a temple or any place of worship. They may go to churches, gurudwara, mosque; temples on a regular basis may be daily or weekly depending on their convenience. It all depends on individual mind set and many a time upbringing plays an important role. There is yet another group who never believe in God and they never step in a place of worship.

This is a story of such a person who never believed in the existence of God. This was Dr Giriraj, a famous cardiac surgeon; he was highly qualified with many foreign degrees to his credit. He was very skilful and precise in his operative procedures. He was so good that there was not even a single failure in the operations that he performed. Therefore, he was the most sought-after surgeon. It was very difficult to get his appointment too. He was very good in paediatric cardiac surgery too.

However, he never believed in God. He used to say that "I believe in my capacity and the confidence in me, in what I learnt and what was taught to me. My job is to give the best to my patients". Where does the God fit in here? However, his wife Pooja was totally opposite to him and strongly believed in God. She had a room for worship i.e., a puja room and she was very regular with it and methodical. Fortunately, her husband never objected to what she was doing but never stepped into puja room.

One fine day, parents with their lovely girl child stepped into the consultation room with prior appointment. After going through all the reports Dr Giriraj examined the girl in detail, then he turned to the parents and said this little girl needs operation and gave a complete account as to how long it will take to operate and how many days she may have to be there in the hospital. Generally, doctors explain the risk involved in such type of intricate operation. However, Dr Giriraj never mentioned anything about it, as he had never encountered any problems. That was the confidence in himself and in his team.

After the consultation was over and when they were ready for the operation, he directed them to get admitted and to be in touch with his assistants. As they were about to leave the little smart girl Aarushi said to the doctor "Sir, can I ask you a question" Dr Giriraj was surprised and amazed and appreciated the boldness of little girl.

Aarushi asked Doctor "are going to open my heart"

Doctor: Yes, baby.

Aarushi: My Mom and my teacher have told me that God dwells in everyone's heart, is it?

Doctor: May be my dear.

Aarushi: When you open my heart, please see how God looks like. I love him so much and would like to know from you as to how he looks.

Doctor: Done baby! It's my promise and I shall certainly tell you.

Aarushi: With her folded hands, looked into the eyes of the doctor and said, "thank you very much".

Doctor: Don't worry baby, you will be given the detailed account about the God whom you love you.

Dr Giriraj never wanted to displease her and went on telling yes. Aarushi went home happily and came back to hospital on the day she was fixed for operation. On the day of admission, all investigations were done and posted her for surgery the next day as 1st patient. Next day, Dr. Giriraj, with all his confidence, entered the operation theatre. As usual the assistant would open the chest and leave the rest to the boss and after the surgery is over the assistant would close the chest.

A very confident Dr. Giriraj completed the procedure in the perfect manner, took off his gloves and asked the assistants to close the chest as usual. In the meantime, the anaesthesiologist said "Sir, her BP is falling, and she is turning blue even with oxygen". This was a great surprise to Dr Giriraj as he had never encountered such an event. He couldn't understand what was going wrong as the surgery was neatly done. He wanted to see whether there was any bleeding inside or anything else had gone wrong. As the anaesthetist started pushing necessary drugs to help the child Dr. Giriraj put the gloves on again and opened the chest himself. Everything was very clear and there was nothing wrong. He held the tiny heart in is hand and started squeezing it, but nothing seemed to help. Then without realising, he said Oh God! help me and remembering the words of the little child that God dwells in the heart, he held the heart with his both hands and closed his eyes, as if he was in prayer. He probably knew no prayer but what was in his mind, God only knows. As he was holding the heart in his hands many of the pictures of the God in the Puja room in his house where his wife used to pray, passed his memory lane. As if a miracle happened, the heart started beating and the BP started coming up to normal. Fortunately, the child came out of the crisis. There was a sigh of relief and surgeon could smile. With folded hands he thanked God and shifted the little child to paediatric ICU. Generally, Dr Giriraj would not enter the ICU after surgery but for the 1st time he sat in ICU room watching the monitors closely. As this had never happened in his lifetime, all the intensivists and assistants were amazed to see this change. After the child settled, he asked the intensivist to take care of the child and went to the theatre for second operation. So, this was for the 1st time such a thing had happened, and God's name came on his lips. Generally, he would call the patient at the time of discharge to his chamber and give his final advice and instructions. However, there was a difference this time. He visited the lovely little Aarushi who gave a broad smile with her folded hands profusely thanked him. She never forgot to ask Dr Giriraj: "Doctor did you see God in my heart?" He suddenly got up, went close to her, carried and hugged her and said, "yes baby, He was sparkling white with brilliance and radiance which brightened the whole operation theatre". He conveyed his blessings to you and your family. He put her back on the bed and put his hand on her head and left the room and one could see a drop of tear at the corner of his eyes. This arrogant atheist doctor had only believed in his confidence and capacity and nothing beyond.

Now, this incidence had shaken him. He started believing in God and was convinced that there is some super power which is beyond our reach and comes to our rescue when necessary. For the first time, he went home and entered the puja room and put a flower over lord Ishwar. It was a great surprise to his wife to see this transformation. Then onwards one could see Gods' pictures in his consulting room as well as the operation theatre. He never operated on any case without praying with folded hands and bowing his head. He had to explain about this transformation to his wife as to what happened to a little girl on that day, and this was nothing but a miracle. This was certainly beyond his imagination and could not comprehend how such a miracle can happen without the divine intervention.

Then on, the couple spent countless happy days visiting religious places and getting blessings from the almighty. Dr Giriraj, an arrogant, over-confident and self-reliant person was transformed into a humble and compassionate doctor and his practice soared. He was more popular than earlier, and patients loved and adored him. He started believing in the Saying "I treat, and He cures".

WHERE THERE IS HOPE

THERE IS

FAITH

WHERE THERE IS FAITH

THERE IS

HAPPINESS

Little girl saves a little boy

Next to creating a life, the finest thing a man can do is save one's

Abraham Lincon

This is a true story that happened at Mangeshi temple Goa. Lord Mangeshi is an incarnation of Shiva or Ishwar and Bhagvan Mangesh is worshipped by his devotees at Mardol, Goa. It is an approximately 450 years old temple. As the legend goes it is said that the Shiva lingam was on a hillock and a cow used to pour its milk on the Shiva lingam which was noticed by few persons and arranged to shift it to the present site i.e., Priol, Mardol and the temple was consecrated with a beautiful Goan architecture.

This beautiful temple is a most attractive tourist spot. This is the most visited temple by tourists and others which has housed salubrious environment surrounded by hills and landscapes and greenery. This Hindu shrine has a lot of spiritual significance. Lord Mangesh is our family deity or Kul devata. Its devotees are spread all over the world including the noted late Lata Mangeshkar and her sisters, the greatest singers of India.

It was under the Portuguese regimen and later was included to Indian sovereignty. I still remember that my dad had to take a permit/visa from Delhi to visit Goa. That was when Portuguese rule came to an end through "Operation Vijay" way back in 1961. It was not that easy to enter Goa soon after liberation. For the first time, we entered with the permit/visa we could see the bridges were blown and Indian military had made stop gap arrangements to cross the river. Likewise, there were many hurdles one could face to reach the Mangeshi temple. The Mangeshi temple has its rooms for the devotees and the devotees belonging to Mangeshi temple could stay there. We performed the spiritual pujas and really enjoyed the calm serene atmosphere with positive vibes in the temple. In the presence of God, we could keep ourselves calm and rejuvenate our energy. Since it was our Kul devata or deity, we were allowed to enter sanctum sanctorum and perform puja. The beautiful linga right in the centre of the sanctum sanctorum has an "OM" (ॐ) which is naturally carved one. There are various types of pujas which are classified as Abhishek, Laghu Rudra, Maharudra etc. Ten Abhishek is equal to one Laghu Rudra and 10 Laghu Rudra is equal to one Maharudra. Maharudra is the highest puja that one can perform. There is lot of waiting to perform this Maharudra and it may take 6-8 years to get their turn to perform this puja.

One should really appreciate time management of Mangeshi temple management committee. Exactly at 1pm they perform the afternoon pooja and in the evening the bhajan programme is organised. Every Monday and on some other special days the Pallakki (Palanquin) perambulation around the temple takes place. At the end of the perambulation again Aarati to God is performed. Generally, the attendees to such pujas though late in the night, range from 500-800 people and the whole area is full of devotees and then the prasadam is distributed to all the devotees.

Fortunately for us, our forefathers or ancestors had planned to have Maharudra pooja during first four days of Navaratri. Thus, our family is very fortunate to perform the highest seva on a regular basis which others must wait for years.

It used to be a routine practice to offer flowers and fruits for the prasadam. We regularly brought fruits from Ponda city, nearby. It is a pleasure to clean the fruits, cut it into pieces and put it in a bowl for distribution. It was a usual practice that we used to take a room in the premises, clean the room and put a mat and all the household people are engaged to cut the fruits meant for more than 500 people. We used to take them and give it to archaks to be offered to God and then distribute it to devotees as prasadam.

One day when we went to the temple and after taking the darshan got the room and got all the necessary fruits and everyone sat on the ground to cut fruits into pieces and the grapes to be separated from the bunches. It was my mother Kusumatai, my wife Kavita and my younger sister Veena doing that work.

I was taking bath and getting ready to go for puja. My daughter Rasika who was around four years and son Kavan around two years old were sitting on the table and playing. This room was on the 1st floor and the table was adjacent to window. The windows had no grills, and it was thought the window was locked, but it was not the case. My son Kavan got up and banged the window and alas! The window got opened and he was thrown out. This scene was witnessed by my sister, and she shouted followed by my wife and my mother. In the meantime, my daughter, little older than Kavan reflexively grabbed his legs and as he was dangling down the window. My wife Kavita jumped into action and pulled him up from dangling position into the room. This scene was observed by the devotees on the ground, and they too started shouting.

If he had fallen straight from the first floor, he would have hit the tiled ground and would have certainly sustained head injury and anything could have happened. Then the chances of survival would have been bleak. Secondly, Rasika the elder child was also too small, and she could have been thrown out along with my son. One cannot imagine what a tragedy it could have been.

It is remarkable how a small child could react so quickly, grabbing her brother's legs and preventing his fall in a split second. I can say we were in Mangeshi temple and ardent devotees of Lord Mangeshi; it was "He" who saved both my children. It was a good prudence that God could come to our rescue and help to avoid this disaster. By any stretch of imagination, one cannot imagine how this could happen, and it was nothing short of miracle. Thus, my faith in God had a proof and I say, "God still exists".

It is very certain that in life, even time is not in our hands.

Saving life certainly is not in our hands. Even an eminent doctor may not save a life with all the experience and expertise. We should strongly believe in supernatural power which plays a pivotal role when it comes to saving life.

If we believe in God, yes, it is HE who does that job without our request.

One may believe in one's own capabilities or self-confidence. However, when you are badly stuck, you need certainly to depend on someone who infuses energy, and you can bounce back.

Life is very uncertain; it can take any turn; one must be godly lucky to survive such instances. Prayers always count!!

FAITH IS A LIVING, DARING CONFIDENCE IN GOD'S GRACE, SO SURE AND CERTAIN THAT A MAN WOULD STAKE HIS LIFE ON IT ONE THOUSAND TIMES. THIS CONFIDENCE IN GOD'S GRACE AND KNOWLEDGE OF IT MAKES MEN GLAD AND BOLD AND HAPPY IN DEALING WITH GOD AND WITH ALL CREATURES; AND THIS IS THE WORK OF THE HOLY GHOST IN FAITH.

Martin Luther

Miraculous Escape

Existence of God shouldn't be debated.... It's an opinion from everyone.... but in my best opinion, God is the reason why we're here and if you think not so.... Then your opinion is absurd,

My father Vithal Rao was popularly called Vithal during his childhood and few of his close friends called him Vittu. He was the last child born to Vaikunt Rao. Vaikunt Rao was a landlord at Haliyal. As my father had very curly hair which looked like a basket, he was also called "butti". He was always focused on his studies and probably dreaming to do something big. The story which he narrated goes like this. His father, being a landlord, owned hundreds of acres of land. They had many buffaloes and cows in the backyard. Anyone coming to the house will always leave after breakfast or lunch. Without it they were not allowed to go. They were also offered milk to drink.

In the backyard there were bathrooms, storerooms and a very big open yard too. It was the duty of women folk and children to milk the cow or buffalo and to store it in the steel buckets and later taken inside for boiling and using it. There was also a well from where children used to draw water and take bath after completing the work of milking the cow.

One day Vithal finished his work of getting the milk and kept it next to the storeroom to be taken inside later. Adjacent to it was the bathroom. However, kids enjoyed taking bath in the open. He started taking bath, applied soap but in the meantime the bucket toppled, and all the water fell out of the bucket. As he had already put soap on the face, he went near the bathroom to pick up another bucket filled with water. Instead of going to bathroom side he went near the storeroom and picked up the full bucket, and continued taking his bath, and only realising later, when he opened his eyes that he was pouring milk over himself instead of water. His mother observed that and not only scolded him but slapped him and said, "are you taking a bath or doing Abhishek with milk".

In the course of time, the family relocated to Dharwad. He was a student at Karnataka high school and as he mentioned to us, there was competition between him and Smti. Sarojini Mahishi who went on to become a union minister. Those days, there were hardly four or five engineering colleges, and he got admission in Pune engineering college. After finishing his engineering, he joined a firm, which was into construction of bridges. He was posted to build a bridge in between Yallapur and Karwar which he supervised and completed. Later, the company went into loss and then he decided to join PWD and eventually became the Chief Engineer. He was an irrigation expert who worked in Ghataprabha-Malaprabha, Badra and upper Krishna project. He also served as Chief Engineer assigned to the Kali project. He served as CADA (Command Area Development Authority) administrator for Ghataprabha-Malaprabha projects.

He used to go to Bangalore frequently for various meetings. Once he took his juniors along with him for an important meeting at Bangalore. He was diabetic, was a heavy smoker but a teetotaller. He used to get up for natural calls in the night. As he was travelling in the train probably, he got up in the sleep to go to the toilet and it so happened that instead of opening the toilet door he opened the main door in his sleep and was thrown out of the train. This happened near Kadur between Hubli and Bangalore. It so happened that he was thrown on well grown bushes. He had lots of scratches, wounds cuts on the face and head. Fortunately, he had no fractures anywhere. He was in his pyjama and banian. As he fell, he woke to understand that he has fallen from the running train. It is said that if he had fallen 50 yards ahead the train would be passing through a culvert and lower down there were only big stones; he would have certainly sustained a head injury and multiple fractures. Fortunately, he fell on bushes. It was pitch dark and he could spot a light which was far off from the site where he fell. He didn't have chappals as they probably have been thrown elsewhere. He somehow managed to walk with all the difficulties in the field to reach the spot where he could see the light. It was dead in the night, and he was drenched with the blood, and he was only on banian and pyjama. He reached the place where he could see the light and there were few small houses. He knocked the door of a house and the person who was a farmer and seeing him with blood and scratches and bleeding from the face shut the door. There was no other go than to knock the next door. There came a person who was a schoolteacher who made him to sit and offered him water and learnt the story about what had happened. He mentioned about a health centre where they could walk down to get some treatment. By that time, the morning sunrise was visible, and the teacher and my father reached the health centre. Teacher had no vehicle and those days there were no mobile phones. He reached the government health centre and doctor was requested to attend.

In the meantime, the team travelling with him noticed that "Saheb" was not to be seen in the compartment. They searched the whole bogie. But they noticed that main door open. As soon as they reached Bangalore, he being the Chief Engineer on duty, the police and other higher officers were informed. Immediately the police department, PWD and the Railway department swung into action and asked to patrol the railway track. By this time my father had also sent information to nearby department informing them of his location in Kadorhalli PHC. The search team came to the primary health centre and saw him in a bad state. He had sutures put on the forehead, but blood was oozing from all the grazes. His office staff and police decided to shift him to Bangalore medical centre. It seems my father said he would prefer to go to KMC (Karnataka Medical College) Hubli, where I was doing my post-graduation.

We were all very worried when the news reached us. The only message which we got was Deshpande Saheb fell of the running train, and we are bringing him to the KMC. We were all waiting anxiously and so was the casualty medical officer as he was senior government officer.

Ultimately, when he did arrive in a jeep, he had a ghastly look with bandages on his head, blood stains on the body, face and on his clothes. Fortunately, nothing major had happened. There was no head injury. Immediately, he was attended to and admitted. He was completely investigated and kept under observation. All the department people gathered and started to enquire about his health. This also came in the news daily on the very 1st page titled **miraculous escape of a Chief engineer**. Once he, settled, we shifted him to our house in Dharwad. He went to the district hospital for regular dressings and removal of stitches etc. What is interesting and amazing is although he was a senior chief engineer; he preferred Government medical college and District hospital for his treatment rather than any private hospitals even though we knew many of them personally.

The then PWD minister of Government of Karnataka, Shri D. B. Chandregouda personally visited our house to enquire about his health and welfare.

It was truly a miraculous escape. Imagine, if he had sustained multiple fractures, head injury or a major bleed, we would have lost him before locating him. We were fortunate that it was a sheer prudence that God saved him. Falling from a running train without sustaining any major injuries, reaching a good Samaritan i.e., a teacher's house and then getting treatment in PHC is all God's blessing. He was an eminent engineer, a strict disciplinarian, who never harmed anyone, and all the colleagues adored and respected him. Even now after many decades, his subordinates who worked with him say that they have not seen an officer like him.

It's all grace of God which amply makes it clear that God does exist. If you have helped people and you are loved by people God is there to save you.

HOPE IS BEING ABLE TO SEE THAT THERE IS LIGHT DESPITE ALL OF THE DARKNESS

- Desmond Tutu

MIRACLES HAPPEN TO THOSE WHO BELIEVE IN THEM

- Bernard Berenson

Life is Unpredictable

The world is so unpredictable. Things happen suddenly, unexpectedly. We want to feel we are in control of our own existence. In some ways we are, in some ways we're not. We are ruled by the forces of chance and coincidence.

Paul Auster

Right from birth to death a person goes through many ups and downs. There are hardly a few who had not encountered any problem whatsoever except at a latter period in life one gets into age related problems.

Believe me, if you ask any person "whether he/she had any difficulties during their lifetime, the answer would be most of the times a definite 'yes'. Many will recollect their bad times or even a worst time and how they came out in a miraculous way. Many a time they say, "I had the second birth"! How true it is! Life is a journey on a boat right from getting into the boat or cruise with life jacket and getting seated on your seat. You do not know what is in the store. Many a time the boat gets toppled or halfway through the journey, a cyclone comes heading towards the boat. This was not an exception even to an extraordinary ship like Titanic. No one probably even ever imagined that they are likely to have a mishap but alas that happened and now it is a history.

Similar will be the experience to a family in an aircraft whether it is a Boeing or a helicopter. We enter the flight with confidence, but our life is in the hands of the pilot or the weather conditions or the unforeseen mechanical fault in the aircraft. Many people thank God after they land safely. We have heard of several aircraft accidents wherein we lost some leaders of ours. Madhavrao Scindia, the Maharaja of Gwalior and senior politician lost his life in an accident. Sanjay Ghandhi also had a fatal accident and so also the sitting Chief Minister YSR (Yeduguri Sandinti Rajasekhara Reddy) of Andhra Pradesh met with an accident and died. The latest unfortunate tragedy was the demise of the Chief of Defence Staff of the Indian Armed Forces, General Bipin Rawat in a helicopter crash.

So, life is uncertain whether one is a small or big person with everything in his or her command. As we have heard the stories of people dying in accidents, there are equal numbers of instances where people have miraculously escaped. The destiny is not in our hands. It is certainly controlled by the superpower or the God.

Here is the narration of such a narrow escape and coming out of the jaws of death

CHILD SAVES A CHILD

A true story indeed! This happened in Ghataprabha where my father Vithal Rao Deshpande was serving as an executive engineer. We lived in a big bungalow with a very big garden and fruit bearing trees. This was the building built by the British. Ghataprabha, though a small township was a beautiful place with a reservoir and during monsoon we could see beautiful overflow of water from the dam site. Everywhere there was greenery and a nice breeze. My father was an executive engineer which was the highest post. He was 5'10" tall, a hefty personality and was highly respected because of his sincerity, confidence and an apt administrator, a position he held with dignity. His routine was to get up at 4AM, light his cigar and complete all the pile of files before sunrise. He was a very strict administrator and called spade a spade. His work was very much appreciated by the then PWD minister, Shri Chennabasappa and got him transferred to his own constituency at K R Nagar. That is the way he worked with zeal and enthusiasm.

He was a family man and many of the relatives would visit Ghataprabha and spend some good time in that place. It was a Ganesh festival day and there were many relatives at home and plenty of children. It was on one particular day children started playing and prepared a small figure which they called Ganesh. They pretended as if they were doing puja by offering some flowers from the garden. They had earlier witnessed immersion of Lord Ganesh in the reservoir or river or well. They started emulating that and they took a small procession from one end, someone holding the figure of Lord Ganesh which they had prepared, decorated with flowers and marched towards the pond. There were two ponds in the garden, may be measuring 25 feet x 25 feet and a depth of 1.5 feet. As the children's procession approached the pond, they noticed tuft of hair floating on the water. They screamed and my younger sister Veena who was about 5-6 years old, jumped and could hold the hair and pulled it up. He was my youngest brother who was probably less than 2 years had drowned. Listening to the screams, my mother, my aunt and everyone else rushed. It was a shock to my mother and everyone. They immediately took him inside, put him on his tummy and applied pressure to remove water and gave mouth to mouth breathing as the child was turning blue. In the meantime, my father told Dr M K Vaidya, Chief of KHI hospital who was also his friend and informed him that they were rushing to hospital.

Dr Vaidya was waiting and immediately took the child inside and administered oxygen, medicines etc. Everybody was waiting anxiously outside. After some time, he came out and said that the boy is out of danger. He also said you have picked him up at the right time as he must have fallen a little while ago before pulling him out. As the child was totally drowned except floating hair, another few seconds or minutes, we would have lost the child. It was truly a miraculous escape. It was under the pretext of immersing Lord Ganesh that the kids reached the pond only to find my brother in time, or we would have lost him. It is also the timely medical attention which saved him. One can only say that miracles do happen due to God's blessings, and this amply justifies the saying that **God does exist.** It is not a simple co-incidence. It is an example of the divine intervention. All the family members thanked the children in whom they saw God who gave a 2nd birth to our brother.

Life is not in our hands, be it a child, elderly, a dignitary or a reputed person. Knowingly well, one could be no more next day but still behave as if they are eternal!!

There are umpteen examples of loss of life of a child by drowning. I vividly remember my friend's darling son born after many baby girls, dying in a garden pond. Similarly, a senior police officer's son drowned in a small garden tank, which was supposed to cater to big garden in front of the house.

Kids drown even in a bucket of water. Bigger children and even college going students drown in rivers or sea on many occasions.

It is a parental responsibility to cover all the water tanks in the garden and never keep a bucket filled with water in the bathroom when there are small children at home. Similarly, never allow a child to go into the water unattended. It is equally important to plug the electrical points particularly when they are placed low so that kids cannot reach out and put their little fingers into it. We have seen kids dying of electrical shock. Parents need to be very careful in all these respects. Or, they will have to pay a heavy price for a small mistake.

Providential Escape

In order to go on living one must try to escape the death involved in perfectionism: Hannah Arendt

This is a true story that happened during end of June 2023. My birthday falls on 25th June. We thought of celebrating it in northern India, and finally we narrowed it down to Shimla, Kullu and Manali for the celebration. Truly speaking there is nothing like celebration at this age unlike the one which we celebrated in younger days by cutting cake, having fun and frolic. The difference is to spend time in a peaceful way quietly without any pomp or cake cutting or music etc. and spending time at salubrious atmosphere with beautiful scenery and greenery with calm and peaceful mind away from the routine workload and stress.

We planned it and asked tour operator to give us the options and informed him that it should include 25th June which is my date of birth. He just asked one question "whether you would like to start it on that day or end the tour on that day". What came to my mind God only knows and said plan it in such a way that tour ends on 25th. Thus, he planned our tour, starting from Bangalore and back to Bangalore on 26th June, covering Chandigarh, Kullu, Manali and Shimla. The first half was at Chandigarh wherein we visited the famous Rock Garden, the Mughal Garden, Rose and Butterfly parks and many more which were of importance and proceeded to Manali. The roads were passing through the hills, and they were along the Beas River which was flowing silently. All through there were boats, water sports, paragliding, hot water balloon etc. we passed through many tunnels which were recently inaugurated by the Prime Minister. Similarly, we went to Manikaran, the Gurudwara Shrine and many site seeing places in Kulu Valley and Shimla. As expected, the tour ended in the beautiful city of Shimla where a nice hotel at the top of a hill overlooking the beautiful Shimla was booked for us on my birthday. We went to the beautiful Hanuman Temple at the highest peak of Shimla where big statue of Hanuman was erected, and this was truly inspiring. At the end of our tour after visiting beautiful places at Himachal Pradesh, we left Shimla to reach Chandigarh by Car. There was only little drizzle on 24th June evening at Simla but all through we had beautiful weather on the way back. As we just entered Chandigarh it started pouring but our flight was on time and reached Bangalore and our hometown Dharwad.

After reaching home we saw the news on TV and read in news daily that there was a heavy rainfall in Himachal Pradesh. The Beas River which was so calm and flowing silently when we had visited, had shown its colour and was furious. Due to heavy rainfall there was land slide, the bridges collapsed, and the roads had given way by the force of the water coming from the hills. The Kulu to Manali highway was blocked and stopped for the vehicles. The Manikaran where we had excellent Gurdwara Darshan was also flooded with water. The Salli valley through which we passed many times was greatly damaged by the floods.

These were all the places we had travelled through and looking back we skipped a heartbeat and felt how lucky we were to reach safely without getting stuck anywhere or falling prey to the disaster. It was heart-breaking to see many cars floating on water and several buildings collapsed in those areas. If, we had not opted to end the tour on the 25th of June and instead started the tour on that day, we would have been the victims of this disaster. God only saved us; and we were greatly lucky.

It is yet another narrow escape which we cannot forget. Truly, it was providential escape and nothing else. When this story was uploaded on Facebook, there were many friends who thanked God and said that we were truly lucky, and it is sheerly because you are being good to others and serving the tiny tots with devotion. Your good deeds have helped you. I was touched by the sentiments expressed. It is truly God's wish and the good-will of close friends. With this incidence, it again proves that God does exist.

NO MATTER THE NATURAL DISASTER I'VE COVERED, WHETHER IT'S A WILDFIRE OR FLOOD, I ALWAYS COME BACK WITH A MUCH GREATER PERSPECTIVE: Ginger Zee

CHAPTER III

MY JOURNEY IN MEDICAL PRACTICE

My Journey in Medical Practice

MEDICAL PRACTICE IS FAST CHANGING.

INDIVIDUAL PRIVATE HOSPITALS WILL BE A THING OF THE PAST IN THE DAYS TO COME

The practice of medicine is an art, not a trade; a calling, not a business; a calling in which your heart will be exercised equally with your head.

To study the phenomenon of disease without books is to scale an uncharted sea, while to study books without patients is not to go to sea at all.

Sir William Osler

In Medicine, if you want to remain where you are then you need to run to keep abreast of changing medicine.

Medical practice has completely revolutionized itself. The reasons are many:

* Modern technology

* Expectation of patients

*Affordability and cost effectiveness

*Need for stress-free life for doctors.

With advent of specialists and super specialists the patient care has certainly improved but the personal touch has taken a back seat.

A WAY FORWARD FOR A MEDICAL GRADUATE

Every doctor prefers to be in the Metropolitan cities. There are plenty of super specialists in big towns. Whether they are all doing well is a million-dollar question. They do not prefer to be in two and three tier cities.

Many doctors do not dare to be in private practice. There could be many reasons. They firstly prefer to be attached to a Medical College. It is a big shelter, and they feel comfortable. Few may opt to have an additional private practice which is a bonus to them.

Few others join corporate hospitals to try their luck, and few prosper, and others sail through.

Yet another aspect is a group practice, where in few specialists come together and start a multi-disciplinary hospital. They pool in their money and take some loan and get going. If there is good understanding amongst the partners, then it will not only survive but flourish. Otherwise, it will fail.

There is yet another concept where in a moneyed person invests and gives attachment to specialists. This may also work if the management is on sound footing and have a high credibility.

IN THE PRESENT CIRCUMSTANCES WHETHER INDIVIDUAL DOCTORS CAN START THEIR OWN HOSPITAL?

This is a tricky question to answer. In big cities, it is the thing of the past. However, in small cities they do start but have lots of limitations. Even though a specialist can take risk and venture into major operations or ICU care, it is too demanding and stressful. So, majority of them prefer to have lone practice.

In the past there were many hospitals managed by consultants. Many of them are single specialty hospitals. In the present-day practice with lots of expectations from patients and availability of medical college and corporate hospitals, we do not see such of individual hospital anymore.

However, let me share my experiences of starting a single specialty hospital during 1978.

I started with just a five-bedded hospital and gradually developed into a 100-bed exclusive Paediatric hospital at Dharwad.

The story is exciting, and it needs complete dedication and commitment. We, the old generation doctors were lucky to have complete faith and trust in the treating doctors.

Now, things are different. Everyone comes with a sort of suspicion and there are plenty of Google doctors. It is now not that easy as it was in the past.

Now a days, individuals starting independent hospitals is a rare phenomenon. Of late, it is all multispecialty hospitals which are started by a group of doctors or corporate hospitals, wherein doctors are employees. The pleasure of having your own hospital is great; at the same time, the headache that one gets into at times is greater than the happiness. All administrative work, managing employees and materials happen to be the owner's responsibility. One cannot leave the hospital and go anywhere as there will be no one else to take care. Thus, the owner is tied to his hospital relinquishing his personal pleasures.

Present day generation doctors do not wish to have such headaches. They want a free time to pursue their hobbies and do not wish to get entangled in the administrative work. They prefer to be a free bird without any personal attachment anywhere.

In view of this, the individual owned hospitals are not coming up anymore. With the change of mind-set of the new generation doctors, no one wants to take a risk, and any problematic patients are referred to medical colleges or corporate hospitals. The days are not when no individual private hospitals would exist.

THE BEST DOCTOR GIVES THE LEAST MEDICINES

Benjamin Franklin

FIRST EVER CHILDREN'S HOSPITAL STARTS IN A HUMBLE WAY.

It was 27th December 1978, the first ever exclusive children's hospital starts in Dharwad a District Head Quarter.

There was a block in the house which was converted into this little hospital which had a separate staircase.

There was a consulting Chamber, a small reception counter, a procedure room, five beds and a cosy waiting hall.

It was inaugurated by the then doyen of medical field Dr D V Nadkarni who was the former dean of Karnatak Medical College.

I told him about starting my own hospital and wished to seek his blessings.

There was a simple, small white invitation card with no name of the chief guest.

I invited him to inaugurate the hospital. To this he replied "You never said that I am supposed to inaugurate it. Otherwise, I would have applied some roses paste on my cheeks, some make-up, and worn perfumes before coming".

He had come in white trousers and white half bush-shirt and a handkerchief hanging from the buttons in the front. (I do not know why the handkerchief)

He put his right foot forward and saw the facilities of the new hospital and blessed me. We also performed Satyanarayan puja.

It was a simple opening ceremony with well-wishers and doctor friends. It was totally unlike the present-day grand inauguration, without pomp & piety.

OLD TIME PRACTICE

In those days, the gadgets that we have now, were not available. That time there were no CT scans, MRIs or even ultrasound machines.

How difficult it was without the sophisticated equipment! We had an X-ray machine and a side lab for routine tests.

The diagnoses revolved entirely on the clinical judgements.

I wonder now, but it is true, that in those days, I did subdural tap (drawing fluid from the anterior fontanels), drained liver abscess, pericardial effusion (fluid collected around the heart), bone marrow aspiration and many more. Now we do not do those procedures unless supported by gadgets and done by experts in that field.

One may be surprised to note that we did not have disposable IV cannula or sets. We used to boil rubber tube and connect them to the dropper and fix it to an IV needle. Again, those days IV cannula was not available, and we used to use regular hypodermic injection needles. I had brought some imported IV cannula from Bombay for the use in new-borns.

That was the type of practice we did then. Diagnosis was made by clinical acumen. Stethoscope was a great tool then, but its importance is lately dwindling.

Practice was new to me. In our curriculum we were not taught how to practice.

I am happy to learn that National Medical Mission is introducing subjects like interpersonal relations, communication skills, counselling etc. These are essential tools for any doctor and more so for a private practitioner.

I still remember the golden advice my father gave me before I started my practice.

WORDS OF WISDOM

1) Never leave your chamber during consulting hours. He said the availability of a doctor is of paramount importance than your qualifications. Since we were in the same block he used to send his daughter in law i.e., my wife who was just married with a cup of coffee. It was an excellent time for both of us to know each other. We used to have more coffee than patients. It was like "Coffee pe charcha".

It was equally true that "A lot can happen over a cup of coffee" a tag line of Coffee Day!!

2) Never be after money. God has given you enough and you care for patient's satisfaction. Their blessings will take you a long way.

3) Be nice to every patient and never get angry with any one at any time.

4) Be humble at all times. Arrogance has no place.

5) Take care of poor patients. If they do not have money to buy medicines give samples and help them to buy. You may wave off your fees.

Those golden words still ring in my ears, and I follow them even now.

MY FIRST EVER NIGHT CALL

My hospital was inaugurated on 27th December 1978.

It was strange that very next night at around 10 pm, I got a call from the hospital that a seriously ill child has come.

All those relatives who came for the inauguration were amazed to know how an emergency comes so early in practice.

As the hospital was on the first floor, I rushed to see the first ever night call.

Parents said that the child was sick for some time, he had been vomiting and had difficulty in breathing. By the time child was brought to my hospital, boy was limp with no respiratory effort. There were no heart sounds. I tried to resuscitate but to no avail. It was a 'brought dead' baby. I explained to the parents, and they left.

I was extremely disappointed that the first baby as an emergency to the hospital was 'brought dead.' When I returned home everyone was excited and curious to know as to what the case was.

I told them that it was a dead baby. Everyone's enthusiasm was dampened and nothing to say. My 75 years old aunt from Mumbai said, that any new hospital must wait for months to get an emergency in the night; you got it on the very first day! God will bless you, do not worry.

That was the beginning of my journey, strange but true. As per my aunt's prediction, God has been kind to me.

Would be physician turns to be a Paediatrician.

Those days, interviews were held in our medical colleges for selecting the post-graduation seats.

My interview went very well. My choice was Paediatrics, but I was given a seat for MD (Medicine). There was no way out, so I joined and was posted in Dr Hande's unit.

Other units were headed by Dr NK Channappa, Dr Jadhav, and Dr M Maiya.

Every month a clinical meeting was held by all the four units.

Though I was a first year PG (Postgraduate), my boss chose me to present a case. I vividly remember that other unit PGs were either final year, or second year students and I was the one from the first year. I remember that I presented a case of " Unstable Angina".

I had prepared it well as it was an opportunity and did well in discussions too. Dr Hande complimented me.

After I completed three months in the medicine department, Dr Krishna who was a first year PG in Paediatrics approached me for a swap. He knew of my interest in

Paediatrics, and he was keen on doing Medicine. I agreed and we went to our Principal Dr N. K. Channappa who was also the HOD of Medicine. Dr Krishna explained about the exchange of departments. Dr Channappa stared at me and said in Kanada "Yakakppa Medicine serudilwa? ("You do not like Medicine?)

With a meek voice I said Sir, my first priority was Paediatrics. He took the application from both of us and forwarded it to the Vice Chancellor with his recommendations.

Later, I was suggested to see Mr CJ Kamalani, a senior person and a Syndicate member having good connections in the university.

I met him at his residence, A tall, fair, and handsome person welcomed me and said to take a seat. I was hesitant to sit in front of him as a medical student. He made me feel comfortable and I sat at the corner of a sofa. He got all the details and said it should not be a difficult as there is a mutual agreement. He called his stenographer for dictation and gave his recommendations. He also spoke to Vice Chancellor directly.

Finally, our request was granted. It was much easier those days. Thus, I joined department of Paediatrics under Prof Dr M Jayaram.

Dr Krisna joined Medicine, and he is settled in Chickmangalur.

MD EXAMINATION, A NIGHTMARE.

MD examination is not a cakewalk. It is tough and the passing rate those days was exceptionally low. Examiners were strict and expected students to reach good standards.

My boss used to say "When we give you an MD degree, this means that we are giving you a crown. Be prepared well".

Thus, only few could clear in the first attempt. We were three students sitting the examination. We worked under four Professors and HODs. Dr M Jayaram, Dr Ankegouda, Dr Indira Amla, and Dr D B Meundi.

Dr Ankegouda had a favourite student who was a diligent worker and intelligent too.

He used to say that even if the toughest examiner comes from any corner of India, he will surely be the first to pass. This used to give goose bumps to me and the other candidate.

We had two external examiners, one Dr Indirabai from Tirupati and the other Dr Y C Mathur from Hyderabad. Madam was supposed to be very tough.

Those days, examiners used to correct the papers and ask questions on our answers too.

As the train in which the examiners travelled was inordinately delayed, I gave my viva Voce at midnight. Everybody was tense but I tried to be calm.

There was one long case and two short cases.

The result does not depend on how much you have read or the knowledge you have accumulated; it is how you interpret the case and how nicely support your answers to the various questions posed by examiners. It depends on your luck, presence of mind and how calm you remain.

I was giving answers coolly and the few sentences which I uttered impressed the examiners and the theory papers which they corrected and the queries from them were adequately answered.

It was tradition to announce the results without delay.

We were in the hostel with all of us were anxious and tense. The first information that came to us was that only one candidate has passed!

We knew it must be the favourite of Prof. Ankegouda. That made us further jittery. Finally, after some hours, came the news that I was the only one to clear the exam. What a sigh of relief? We all three hugged each other, after all we were friends studying together for a long time in the medical college.

It was a literally a nightmare as we took the exam at dead of night.

I thank almighty for his blessings.

WHENEVER THE ART OF MEDICINE IS LOVED THERE IS ALSO A LOVE FOR HUMANITY: HIPPOCRATES

My First Home Visit

Poverty Ignorance galore!!!

The test of our progress is not whether we add more to the abundance of those who have more. It is whether we provide enough for those who have too little.

Franklin D Roosevelt

Home visit by doctors was common in the past.

Family doctors or general practitioners used to visit homes on regular basis. They used to carry a 'Doctor's bag' with everything in it, medicines, injections, dressing materials, prescription pads and what not. As the doctor entered the house or the compound, the bag would be carried by the household people as a mark of respect.

When a doctor visits the sick patient, the other family members also start discussing their problems. It was something like buy one and get 3-4 free. The amount was paid once a month.

However, the consultants never visited homes.

Now day's home visits are non-existent.

I still remember our Senior Family Physician, Dr V.V. Pavate narrating many interesting instances.

Dr Pavate's house was near a railway station. Once, he was called in to see an extremely sick child in the early hours of the morning. After reaching home, he found that the child was in good condition with a temperature of only100° F which did not warrant a night call.

Add to it, the father of that child requested the doctor to drop him to the railway station on his way back home....

Dr Pavate obliged but knew that the fellow wanted a ride to the railway station as in those days, there were no autos and Tonga's were only available during the day. Such were the mischievous people taking doctors for a ride!

Similarly, once he was called to visit a person who was on death bed. By the time he drove all the way, he saw another doctor coming out of the house declaring the death of that person. Dr Pavate was not even noticed by anyone and those who did see him, disappeared in the crowd and he had to return.

I was a beginner, and I too faced such a situation. I was three months into my practice, and as I was entering the OPD, a person with Dhoti banyan, black beard and moustache came running and said "doctor sahib, my wife has just delivered at home, and the baby is not doing well. Please come immediately.

I felt pity on him and decided to go. I too was excited as it was my first ever home visit. I had a fiat car, and I was driving myself.

I asked the farmer to sit in the car. He was hesitant to sit next to me and opened the rear door and sat. Car etiquettes demand that if the owner is driving one should sit in the front. How can one expect this etiquette from a farmer? I chose to drive and reach the destination. He took to me to Kamalapur area, a suburb of Dharwad. He directed me to go further; the township was over after which a small single road in the village started and the last house was his. I knew

I cannot even turn the vehicle in that very narrow road. Bullock carts were parked on both side of the road.

As I entered his house, it was a certainly different scene. Buffalos and calves were there with fodder and a water tank. There was an elevated platform. There were no doors to the house. Only roof and few walls with bricks which were not even plastered.

The lady who delivered was sleeping on that elevated platform. The placenta and the baby were outside on the floor. This scene was not expected by me. In fact, it was a shock of my life to see this scene.

My bag had a stethoscope, tape, torch, tongue depressor, knee hammer and nothing else. It was not the usual Doctors' Bag' of yester years.

I took courage and asked him to bring something to cut the umbilical cord. The guy went inside and brought a sickle. I said it would not work, and I said to bring a blade. As that fellow had a beard, and no blade was available. He asked me to wait, ran out of the house, and got it from a neighbour. How do you sterilize it?

I asked for spirit knowingly that it may not be available. He went inside and got a bottle of Dettol. I had no option but to sterilize it with Dettol, and again, fortunately, a thread could be procured, which I dipped into the Dettol, cut the cord with the blade, and tied the cord with the available thread.

I asked for a clean cloth, and he gave a towel. I wrapped the baby and as the baby was not breathing properly and him to get the baby admitted to a District Hospital. The father and others fell to my feet and requested me to take this baby to my hospital and do the best. I was in a fix. I agreed and asked them to get into the car. I had to reverse the car. There was a person guiding me and chasing out the sleeping buffalos on the road. It was a testing time for my driving abilities. My God I reached the main road after a herculean task.

The baby was kept in NICU (Neonatal Intensive Care Unit) as his condition was serious with low glucose level and early sepsis. It was a great responsibility to pull the baby out of crisis.

As I struggled to do things which I had never done any time before, the poor people were not only innocent but very humble.

The baby remained in the hospital for 14 days.

Although the bill was not big in amount, the parents could not afford it.

The baby's father and the grandparents entered my consultation chamber and told their plight.

They told me that I was God sent as I saved their baby. The Grandfather said that the baby's father worked as a "geetada alu" i.e., a man is given to a family for working almost free of cost as the family could not pay off debts or loan. This was in vogue those days.

He offered some money to me. I could see the notes of smaller denomination suggesting that it was their hard-earned money. I knew it was difficult for them to look after the baby with no money. I was touched and moved by their simplicity, humbleness and above all the gratitude.

I waived everything, returned the money, and said that they can use it for their baby. They were grateful and emotional.

It was my first ever home-visit and I saw what poverty was and how humble persons could be.

This visit taught me lessons of life and changed my attitude towards the poor with better understanding and care. The blessings of the elders have certainly helped me to feel happy and proud for bringing joy to the poor family, in a small way.

ACCESS TO BASIC QUALITY HEALTH CARE IS ONE OF THE MOST IMPORTANT DOMESTIC ISSUES FACED BY THE DEVELOPING NATIONS.

Tricky Situations at Hospital.

Statistically speaking there is 65 percent chance that the love of your life is having an affair. Be very suspicious.

Scott Dikkers

Hospitals are places where a patient is admitted for necessary treatment for various ailments. Sometimes, it is an emergency and needs immediate hospitalization, which could be in an ICU.

In other circumstances, when a treating doctor feels that outpatient treatment may not be good enough and patient needs further evaluation, then also a patient is admitted.

There are umpteen reasons for admissions, but majority of the patients do not need it. However, there are black sheep in any profession, and unnecessary admissions are common.

In my practice, I did encounter a peculiar situation as regards admission.

A lady from a village brought her son with a high fever with convulsions, and the child was admitted on priority basis. The child recovered fully and was discharged with counselling and advice on precautions to be taken at the time of fever as the seizures or convulsions were due to high fever. The lady went home happily, thanking everyone.

After a spell of time, she came with the same child again with fever. This time fever was not high, and after the necessary investigations was done, the mother was informed that there was no major problem, she could take the child home and give the medications as prescribed.

The village lady stood for a while silently and then said, “Dr Sir, I come from a far-off village, and I do not wish to take a chance with my only son and prefer him to be admitted. “I don't want him to throw convulsion again”. It was a reasonable thinking and some logic in it. Hence, I admitted the child for observation. He was fine within 24 hrs and considered fit for discharge. The mother persisted that she would prefer to stay for a day or two more till he is totally cured. Though it was not necessary, the child was kept for two days more and then sent home.

After three months, the lady brought her son with diarrhoea. The child was looked fine and playful with no dehydration. I wrote the medications and asked her to come after two days for review. Again, she put up her argument that she is from a far-off village and there is no proper transportation and preferred to get admitted despite my suggestion that it wasn't necessary.

I admitted the child. However, I had my own doubts as to why she insists on admission every time. I instructed the admin and staff to keep a proper vigil on this lady.

Our clever nurses came to me the next day and informed me that after the admission of her son, a guy comes late in the evening and stays with her till morning after her husband leaves. She addresses him as her cousin. She always preferred a private room even though she was a village lady.

Then I understood as to why that lady insisted on admission every time.

To me, it came as a surprise. She had an affair with some other man and found the hospital as the best place for fulfilling her desires. No one would ever suspect her, and going to the hotel was not an option. The village lady was not only cunning but clever.

She appeared again with her child after a gap of four months. This time again with fever. As usual, she insisted on admission. I clearly told her that the symptoms were mild does not warrant admission, and I shall not admit.

She again narrated her same story if something were to wrong, who will be responsible?

I got annoyed and said that I have CCTV footage as to who comes to your room every time, and should I show it to your husband? If you are ready, then certainly, I shall admit the child.

She was ashamed and put her head down and disappeared from the scene, never to be seen again.

We medical men and women never think that this type of thing could also happen. We are taken for a ride by such people.

We need to be more vigilant for such occurrences.

Infidelity refers to sex outside one's marriage or civil union without the permission of another partner.

Most of the Western countries have it and Thailand tops the list. Followed by USA, Germany, UK while Finland, Spain are said to have the lowest incidence. However, there is no exact statistics related to India, but certainly not at all very uncommon.

PEOPLE WHO CREATE THEIR OWN DRAMA DESERVE THEIR OWN KARMA

Last Birthday Celebrations of a Lovely Boy in ICU.

Count your life by smile, not tears!

Count your age by friends and not years!

It is a true touching story of a young boy who won the hearts of all the staff of our hospital.

Javed (name changed) an eight-year boy was brought to the hospital for fever, general weakness, and red spots on the skin. After a detailed examination, the boy had anaemia, enlarged liver, spleen, and lymph nodes. The red spots were petechiae meaning bleeding under the skin. After all the investigations were done, it was diagnosed to be a case of blood cancer i.e., Leukaemia.

It is not a common disease in childhood, but still, we do come across cases.

He was the only son, and it was difficult to counsel parents that too, from a village.

The very first question that the child's father asked, "Doctor, do even children get blood cancer?"

We convinced the parents for further investigations like bone marrow test etc. He had chest infection which was to be controlled and so also a blood transfusion was necessary for his low haemoglobin.

That child was lively and full of enthusiasm. He had very pleasing manners and used to sit and greet me as soon as I approached him. Instead of me asking how are you?" He was asking me how I was! One day, I told him whether he could teach me Arabic Urdu alphabets? He immediately responded and said, "Why not?" I told him you are my teacher and that if I go wrong, you need to correct me.

He started the alphabets like Alif, Be, Pe, Te, Se etc. He also said, "Unlike English, they write it from right to left. Every day he taught me, and he was my teacher.

Every day before examining him, he would take revisions and used to say, " Ye galat hai" i.e., this is wrong.

This is how he became friendly not only to me but every staff member.

Once he was settled medically, he was referred to Kidwai Memorial Cancer Institute at Bangalore for further management as there were no cancer hospitals nearby. Now, we have many of them in our two and three tier cities.

He used to get admitted for chemotherapy as per their advice. Thus, Javed was a regular visitor to the hospital, and everyone knew him by name.

After a couple of years, he was told that no further active treatment was necessary and palliative treatment was enough.

Parents also had put all their efforts in saving the child but could understand that they had reached a dead-end and left all hopes.

After a couple of months, parents brought Javed, but this time, he was emaciated with only skin and bones. However, his smile and mannerisms were the same.

He had breathing problems, and I felt it would be better to admit him in Paediatric ICU. Parents said, "Doctor, you do not have to make special efforts as we know the outcome. Father said we do not want him to die at home, as we can't see that and secondly, he has developed many friends at your hospital, and he would be happy here".

I told him not to worry about money; we would like to see that he is monitored better. He needed blood transfusion, but parents refused as it would only prolong his misery.

One day the parents said that "tomorrow is Javed's birthday."

I told him that it was our hospital policy that no child should miss celebrating their birthday, just because they are in the hospital. We used to make the arrangements with cake, chocolates, peppermints, and balloons. At that time all children from the wards gather to greet birthday boy or girl. Some parents have expressed in the past that "this was the best birthday celebration of their child".

However, Javed's father said that they were not in a mood to celebrate and asked us not to take the trouble. However, nurses said we will do it in a simple way with cake cutting and not invite all the children (patients). They said if the Medical Director agrees, we can make an exception as celebrations are not done in ICUs. This was agreed upon.

A nice cake was brought by admin and all the staff gathered. He was very weak and had to be supported to sit and mother had to hold him to cut the cake. All the nurses sang the birthday song in chorus. Everyone knew that it was his last birthday, and one could see wet eyes in all. Javed was not in a condition to understand what was going on but gave a small smile.

Though it is a happy moment, but in this case, it was a ritual, and we never wanted his birthday to be missed.

All of them prayed for his health knowingly well what was in store. Parents were really moved and the tears poured profusely from their eyes. This was a birthday with a difference.

The very next day, Javed left all of us. For the family, the only child had left them too early in life. The hospital waived the entire bill as he had become a family member.

A Hertz van was booked. The entire hospital staff gathered to bid good-bye to Javed. Nurses had brought flowers to be placed on Javed's little body.

Javed was a friend of every staff and my Urdu teacher.

We do not see such an emotional scene when a body is taken away from a hospital. Everyone was wiping their tears.

On one wreath it was written by PICU nurses " Tirugi Ba Javed" meaning "Come back Javed".

The mother hugged the nurses tightly. It was an emotional moment as the entire staff assembled to bid farewell to the departed.

In hospitals, deaths are bound to happen but usually, we are not emotionally attached, but in the case of Javed, he was a frequent visitor to the hospital and everyone loved him.

A lovely boy left a vacuum, and all the staff members were talking about him for months together.

Surprisingly, his parents did visit us whenever they came to the city, to express their gratitude.

A doctor gets satisfaction when he does his best and the parents are convinced about his genuine efforts. We do lose patients, but a few linger in our mind always.

ZINDAGI BADI HONI CHAHIYA, LAMBI NAHI!!

LIFE NEEDS TO BE BIG, NOT LONG. SO LONG ONE LIVES, LIVE LIKE A STAR. LEAVE THE WORLD WITH SMILE WITHOUT REGRETS.

The Story of a Philanderer

"To the sexual offender, possession is power, and total possession is absolute power."

Stephen G. Michaud

Affairs

There are plenty of connotations in the word "affairs." There are Ministers for affairs: External affairs, Parliamentary affairs, etc.

What we are looking at it is not related to the large scope of the word "affairs" but getting focused on one aspect of it, namely sexual affairs.

There are seven types when it comes to sexual affairs.

1. Accidental affair
2. Avoidance affair
3. Philanderer affair
4. Emotional affair
5. The split self-affair
6. Exit affair
7. Sex addict affair

These are extra-marital affairs, which are commonly seen and heard. Romantic infidelity is to have romantic or sexual relationships with someone other than husband, wife, or partner.

The most common reasons attributed are low esteem, lack of love, need of variety, neglect, and sexual abuse in early life.

There are umpteen numbers of affairs that happen, particularly in a workplace or any place where intimacy develops after a long acquaintance.

This is generally seen in three types of people with personality traits, namely horny, opportunistic & trusted cheater.

It is a true story of a philanderer which happened in a Mult speciality hospital and was narrated by the chief of the hospital.

A young man riding a bike with his wife as a pillion rider met with a bad accident. His femur- the thigh bone, was badly fractured. He was operated and a rod was inserted in the bone. The whole leg was plastered. He was getting a sponge bath every day and was recovering in a private room.

The senior doctor, after finishing his rounds, was returning to his chamber. It was late in the evening. He heard a sound from a room. As the door was locked; he just peeped into the room from a window wherein the curtain was partially open.

The Senior Consultant had a shock of his life. He saw something which he could have never imagined.

The young man was lying with his plastered leg, and a nurse was seen in an uncompromised position on top of him.

In disbelief, he returned to his chamber and wondered about the type of people that get into the hospital.

OMG!!! Anything can happen in any place. It is after all the mind-set of such persons. It was the same nurse who gave him sponge bath and was trapped by this philanderer to have his enjoyment in a sacred place like hospital. He could not move the whole leg as it was plastered but still managed his way.

God save such perverts!

Unfortunately, such acts bring a bad name to the hospital and the nursing fraternity.

The very next day, the nurse was summoned and suspended with wise counsel.

We do encounter such rare instances in hospitals, which make us put our heads in shame.

SEXUAL PREDATORS WERE LIKE COCKROACHES. FOR EVERYONE YOU SAW, THERE WERE TWENTY MORE HIDING BEHIND THE WALLS.

- ***Karin Slaughter***

Story of Half Pants

Attire will never reflect your personality

There is no one who hasn't worn half pants in his lifetime. Most of the children wear half pants. Even in schools, half pants and half bush shirts tucked inside, and shoes with socks is usually the uniform. The colour and the pattern of the half pants change as per the school norms. During our childhood, we enjoyed wearing half pants throughout the school education. Of late, we have seen a change wherein half pants are replaced by a full pant.

When it comes to adults, we see them wearing half pants on the beaches and some wear at home too. Wearing half pants as regular attire is generally not seen in India in majority of the places. Whereas, in the western culture, we see half pants everywhere including business places and offices.

HALF PANTS IN CLINICS

Doctors generally attend the Continuing Medical Education (CME) programme to enhance the knowledge and to know what is new in the field. There, the latest knowledge is imported by senior and experts and thus doctors learn newer things in medicine. Now it is mandatory by Neonatal Medical Council of India.

In such a CME, a senior paediatrician and the National past president of Indian Academy of Paediatrics was delivering a lecture. He is generally a very humorous speaker and brings out the relevant information for medical men in practice, in teaching or in government service.

Once, he was addressing a seminar wherein he said "Friends, clinical practice is funny and you need to get a hang of it, if you want to be successful". He continued, it is not only the history taking and examining the patient, but it is also important to note how a patient walks into your consultation room and how he behaves. He further added to be careful of the guys entering your chamber wearing half pants. You can take it from me that the person may be an Indian but returning from a foreign country, more likely from the US or Europe.

Why one should be careful is the fact that these gentlemen who used to wear full pant all the time in India, when they reach US for studies or for a job gets transformed into the half pant culture. Wherever he goes, he likes to give an indication that he is foreign returned. One should be equally more careful when he uses slang languages and shrugs his shoulder very often white talking. This is a typical foreign culture. Such persons are generally goggle friendly and they have gone through all the things regarding differential diagnosis for their complaints. He will continue to pose you many questions relevant or irrelevant. He will go out with your prescription in his hand, and you should not be surprised if he comes back to your chamber asking the diagnosis again or whether the drugs are safe for his children. He will ask you whether the antibiotics you have prescribed is really needed. As a paediatrician you may try to convince him that the follicular tonsils are inflamed, and the child does need antibiotics. You may also ask him to get blood investigations done to prove it but he would say that he trusts you but in fact he does not and leaves with all the queries. Sometimes, these guys will go back and forth in the consulting room before ultimately leaving. He further continued that you should be more careful when a guy with half pants enters the consulting room with a laptop.

He did not stop there and said in case you want to admit a child of such a guy, your hospital should be well furnished to accept this VIP guest! You need to have good and clean bed sheets, a clean bathroom with a decent spotless commode. You need to keep sanitizers and change the bed sheets on a regular basis. The house keeping staff should be well informed to clean the room often. Your regular room should be converted to a sort of five-star hotel rooms. Even with the best of services if a cockroach is spotted anywhere, you should not be surprised to find a comment, maybe a nasty one in the reviews. So, the professor said that we should be smart tackle such a show-off. It is also true that there are ample people who are foreign returned but are modest and behave very decently and respectfully. Finally, he said to be just careful when you see a person entering your room with half pants.

Unfortunately, this culture is adopted by our own persons from Information technology and Biotechnology who get umpteen chances of going abroad.

A MAN SHOULD NEVER WEAR SHORTS IN THE CITY. FLIP FLOPS AND SHORTS ARE NEVER APPROPRIATE. SHORTS SHOULD BE WORN ON THE TENNIS COURT OR ON THE BEACH.

Tom Ford